741.6 Summers, B. J.
SUM

P9-EEN-487

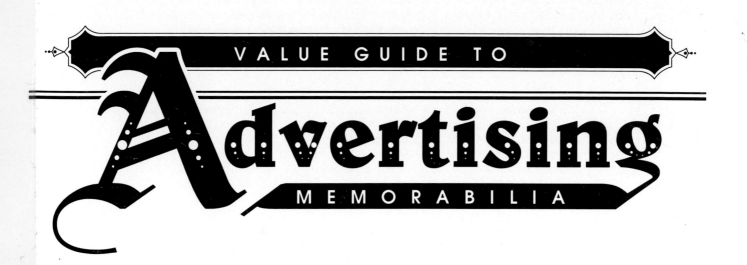

VALUE GUIDE TO Advertising MEMORABILIA

B. J. SUMMERS

PARK CITY LIBRARY

1255 Park Avenue
P.O. Box 668
Park City, Utah 84060
801-645-5140

COLLECTOR BOOKS
A Division of Schroeder Publishing Co., Inc.

The current values in this book should be used only as a guide. They are not intended to set prices, which vary from one section of the country to another. Auction prices as well as dealer prices vary greatly and are affected by condition as well as demand. Neither the Author nor the Publisher assumes responsibility for any losses that might be incurred as a result of consulting this guide.

On the cover: Pepsi sign/BE SOCIABLE..., $95.00. Coca-Cola tray/red-head girl, $200.00. Mr. Peanut figure, peanut butter maker, $30.00. Dairy Brand tin/NEW YORK VANILLA ICE CREAM, $20.00. Lance glass jar/FROM THE HOUSE OF LANCE, $65.00. Gordon's glass jar/"TRUCKS SERVING THE BEST," $125.00. Union Farmer's Gin, glass scene thermometer, $30.00. Winston thermometer/TASTES GOOD...LIKE A CIGARETTE SHOULD, $30.00. Old Hickory Distillery crock/MADISONVILLE, KENTUCKY..., $150.00. Prairie Farms clock/MILK, ICE CREAM, $75.00.

SEARCHING FOR A PUBLISHER?

We are always looking for knowledgeable people considered to be experts within their fields. If you feel that there is a real need for a book on your collectible subject and have a large comprehensive collection, contact us.

COLLECTOR BOOKS
P.O. Box 3009
Paducah, Kentucky 42002-3009

Cover design by Beth Summers.
Book design by Gina Lage.

Additional copies of this book may be ordered from:

Collector Books
P.O. Box 3009
Paducah, Kentucky 42002-3009
or
B. J. Summers
233 Darnell Road
Benton, KY 42025

@ $18.95. Add $2.00 for postage and handling.

Copyright: B. J. Summers, 1994

This book or any part thereof may not be reproduced without the written consent of the Author and Publisher.

Printed by IMAGE GRAPHICS, INC., Paducah, Kentucky

DEDICATION

This book is dedicated to my family. They somehow put up with me throughout the research and assembling of this project. And most of all I dedicate this book to my wife, Beth. She was my computer person and without her help, patience, and understanding this project couldn't have been completed.

CREDITS

Many thanks to the following for their valuable contributions, either by supplying photographs or allowing their collectibles to be photographed:

Affordable Antiques Inc., Oliver S. Johnson/David McCowan, 3480 Wayne Sullivan Drive, Paducah, KY 42001, (502) 442-4992

Affordable carries a general line of antiques and collectibles on Paducah's I-24 loop. Oliver & David run a good mall and if they don't have what you're looking for they can usually find it for you.

Antiques Cards & Collectibles, Ray Pelley, President, 203 Broadway, Paducah, KY 42001, (502) 443-9794

Three floors of antiques and collectibles in an old historic hardware store in downtown Paducah on the Ohio River. A balcony features sports cards and collectibles. Ray's business is just one block off the I-24 loop.

Creatures of Habit, Natalya Hayden & Jack Cody, 403 Jefferson, Paducah, KY 42001, (502) 442-2923

This business will take you back in time with a great selection of vintage clothing and wonderful costumes. Natalya and Jack also offer a variety of great advertising collectibles. One block off the I-24 loop in downtown Paducah.

Collector's Auction Service, Mark Anderton/Director, Sherry Mullen/Manager, Route #2 Box 431, Oakwood Drive, Oil City, PA 16301, (814) 677-6070

Collector's Auction Service specializes in quality oil and gas collectibles. However each auction also has a good line of general advertising. Mark and Sherry direct a great phone auction.

The Depot, I-40 @ Exit 258, Gordonsville, TN 38563, (814) 677-6070

Situated just off I-40 at Gordonsville, The Depot has a general line of antiques and collectibles all situated in the quaint setting of actual train cars!

Franks Antiques & Auctions, Box 516, Hilliard, FL 32046, (904) 845-2870

Frank's offers a general line of merchandise and auction services. His auctions have had a wonderful variety of quality items.

The Green Door, Stan & Judy Baker, 133 South 3rd Street, Paducah, KY 42001, (502) 575-4905

On the I-24 loop at Kentucky Avenue in downtown Paducah, Stan & Judy's place is easy to find and it's easy to spend lots of time browsing there. Here you've got a good line of antiques and collectibles and one of the finest couples in the antique business!

Giller Auction House, Rolf & Wanda Giller, 405 Jefferson Street, Paducah, KY 42001, (502) 444-6786

Rolf runs a good general line auction weekly, plus an antiques-only auction quarterly. There's been a lot of good advertising hammered down by Rolf and you'll find interesting items in his store as well.

Goodlettsville Antique Mall, 213 North Dickerson Pike, Goodlettsville, TN 37072, (615) 859-7002

With 93 booths under roof, plan on spending plenty of time at this store. They feature a good variety of general line merchandise and collectibles and a great many advertising items.

The Illinois Antique Center, Kim and Dan Philips, 100 Walnut Street, Peoria, IL 61602, (309) 673-3354

Two floors of the best quality and variety of collectibles you'll ever want to find are located here. Overlooking Peoria's waterfront, it will take you most of the day to browse through — and there's always plenty of friendly and helpful staff!

Muddy River Trading Post, Gary Metz, 4803 Lange Lane S. W., Roanoke, VA 24018, (703) 989-0475

Along with having some quality advertising pieces on hand, Gary puts on some great auctions. Wonderful varieties of beverage advertising are a speciality!

Pleasant Hill Antique Mall & Tea Room, Bob Johnson, 315 South Pleasant Hill Road, East Peoria, IL 61611, (309) 694-4040

One day isn't enough time for this stuffed-full warehouse mall. Shop till you drop then stop at the tea room inside the mall for a great breakfast, lunch, or supper! Bob has a great variety of antiques and collectibles.

Michael & Deborah Summers, Paducah, KY

My brother and sister-in-law are also collectors of just about everything! You wouldn't believe the trouble Mike and I have gotten into as a result of some of our auction "treasures" Mike and Deb were a great help and provided needed assistance as I put this book together.

Judy & Larry Van Hoy, Carrier Mills, IL 62917

Larry and Judy seem to have Southern Illinois wrapped up in collecting advertising memorabilia. They were a wonderful source of information as I researched this book.

INTRODUCTION

Advertising Art. Those two words evoke different memories to us all, There is almost a magical power in them to instantly transform us to another time and place. My office is full of this art in the form of porcelain signs, neon signs, posters, tins, crockery, milk bottles, medicine bottles, soft drink bottles, and light-up signs. I like it that way! Its very comfortable to work amid the different colors, shapes, and styles of this art. To some, it will bring memories of an old general store with all of its brightly colored advertising items. While to others, it will bring a quick glance at a recent vacation to mind. The use of advertising art as decoration has always had its place, but recently there seems to be a real demand for these articles. It is a wonderful and exciting trend in recycling!

Advertising artists must bring outstanding design and wonderful colors together in a small format to instantly sell the product. This could explain why this form of art is so appealing to so many. When I look at a piece of this art I am attracted not only to its age but the image it conveys. To me this is what makes a piece collectible. It may be truly antique or as recent as a GULF sign.

As the demand goes up so do prices. Some collectors pay thousands of dollars for rare items, while a large portion of these collectibles are still very affordable and if you really search can be bought for only a few dollars. This book is meant to be a guide of what is out there today and is still affordable to the general public. Not all pieces herein are antique, but rather — collectible. The criteria I use for collecting is: If you like it, if the colors are pleasing to you, if the design really catches your eye, then collect it!

CONTENTS

PRICING

Pricing is an especially tough area. There really doesn't seem be be any universal or regulated method of pricing that will suit everyone. Remember, as in real estate, location-location-location plays an important part in collectibles pricing. From east coast to west coast and through the heartland pricing varies according to local popularity of a particular collectible. For example a 16¼" x 14" porcelain Public Telephone sign in very good shape can still be found in my location for around $100.00 in Antique stores, but I've seen the same item in other locations at double that price. This same item should be cheaper at a yard sale or auction. Often prices paid at an auction reflect how much a collector wants an item rather than the actual value of it. Those of you who have been to auctions know what I'm talking about!

Condition will also have a major role in pricing. This same Public Telephone sign that we have talked about has the $100.00 value also because it is in good shape. If it had rust, bullet holes, or dents the value could drop by half or more depending on how much of the sign is obscured.

Knowing the approximate age of a collectible plays a big part in the price it will bring. Dates do appear on a great many advertising items. However, there are some items that do not have a date, only a patent number. The table on page 9 is a patent number listing with corresponding year of production to aid you in dating your collectible.

Buying an item in a retail or wholesale atmosphere will also affect the price. Auctions or yard sales should reflect a wholesale price. But if you have been attending either of these two, you know how much effort it takes to find a particular collectible. You may be better off paying a retail price in a store and foregoing all the time and

work involved in the wholesale arena. Remember when you pay that retail price, you have paid the dealer for the tedious chore of finding, buying, cleaning, researching, and displaying this merchandise.

I have developed the following pricing index to show exactly how I have arrived at the values of the items in this book.

(D) Dealer Price, expect to pay this amount in an antique and collectibles shop.

(B) Auction Bid Price, the amount an item was actually sold for at auction.

(B*) Auction estimated Bid Price, the amount an auction house advertises as expected for a particular item in an up-coming auction.

(C) Collector's Price, the amount a collector has set for an item in his collection. Remember here that an item may have been in a collection for some time and the price paid to acquire it may not be up to today's rapidly changing prices.

There are also some items in this book that are reproductions and have become collectible again! Any of these items will be clearly marked if known. When a particular advertising item is so hot in retail, such as Coke trays, often reproductions are manufactured. Then as the reproductions go off the primary market, they come back in the secondary market as collectibles.

Year	Patent #	Year	Patent #	Year	Patent #	Year	Patent #	Year	Patent #
		1865	45,685	1895	531,619	1925	1,521,590	1955	2,698,434
1836	1	1866	51,784	1896	552,502	1926	1,568,040	1956	2,728,913
1837	110	1867	60,658	1897	574,369	1927	1,612,700	1957	2,775,762
1838	546	1868	72,959	1898	596,467	1928	1,654,521	1958	2,818,567
1839	1,061	1869	85,503	1899	616,871	1929	1,696,897	1959	2,866,973
1840	1,465	1870	98,460	1900	640,167	1930	1,742,181	1960	2,919,443
1841	1,923	1871	110,617	1901	664,827	1931	1,787,424	1961	2,966,681
1842	2,413	1872	122,304	1902	690,385	1932	1,839,190	1962	3,015,103
1843	2,901	1873	134,504	1903	717,521	1933	1,892,663	1963	3,070,801
1844	3,395	1874	146,120	1904	748,567	1934	1,941,449	1964	3,116,487
1845	3,873	1875	158,350	1905	778,834	1935	1,985,878	1965	3,163,865
1846	4,348	1876	171,641	1906	808,618	1936	2,026,516	1966	3,226,729
1847	4,914	1877	185,813	1907	839,799	1937	2,066,309	1967	3,295,143
1848	5,409	1878	198,733	1908	875,679	1938	2,104,004	1968	3,360,800
1849	5,993	1879	211,078	1909	908,436	1939	2,142,080	1969	3,419,907
1850	6,981	1880	223,211	1910	945,010	1940	2,185,170	1970	3,487,470
1851	7,865	1881	236,137	1911	980,178	1941	2,227,418	1971	3,551,909
1852	8,622	1882	251,685	1912	1,013,095	1942	2,268,540	1972	3,631,539
1853	9,512	1883	269,820	1913	1,049,326	1943	2,307,007	1973	3,707,729
1854	10,358	1884	291,016	1914	1,083,267	1944	2,338,081	1974	3,781,914
1855	12,117	1885	310,163	1915	1,123,212	1945	2,366,154	1975	3,858,241
1856	14,009	1886	333,494	1916	1,166,419	1946	2,391,856	1976	3,930,271
1857	16,324	1887	355,291	1917	1,210,389	1947	2,413,675	1977	4,000,520
1858	19,010	1888	375,720	1918	1,251,458	1948	2,433,824	1978	4,065,812
1859	22,477	1889	395,305	1919	1,290,027	1949	2,457,797	1979	4,131,952
1860	26,642	1890	418,665	1920	1,326,899	1950	2,492,944	1980	4,180,867
1861	31,005	1891	443,987	1921	1,364,063	1951	2,536,016	1981	4,242,757
1862	34,045	1892	466,315	1922	1,401,948	1952	2,580,379		
1863	37,266	1893	488,976	1923	1,440,362	1953	2,624,046		
1864	41,047	1894	511,744	1924	1,478,996	1954	2,664,562		

SIGNS

Throughout time merchants have needed a way to attract the buying public to their individual products. In this way manufacturers have actually shaped our culture by convincing us that we need their product in our lives. Using attention-getting colors, designs, and original (and sometimes provocative) art, these advertisers have produced an overwhelming body of collectible memorabilia. For every advertising piece you see there is an artist who designed it. Advertisers have made it possible for the general public to enjoy magazines, newspapers, television, and radio by paying for their products to be represented in each format. Materials range from porcelain and tin to canvas and paper. Lighting and moving parts bring extra interest and value to this form of collectible. Lighting can blink and flash or make items seem to move. On almost any downtown street at night the main source of light will be from advertising signs. Some signs are as familiar as the Coca-Cola button and some are as obscure as Tube Rose snuff. A Buss auto fuse sign can remind you of the corner gas station only a few blocks from your childhood home. Whatever the reason, these artful treasures are fun to collect.

When looking for these pieces of memorabilia some of the factors to be considered are as follows:

Is the piece in good condition? A great deal of advertising memorabilia was designed for and used out-of-doors. The ravages of years of weathering will undoubtedly reduce the value of such a piece.

What materials were used to produce the piece? Porcelain, tin, aluminum, cast iron, cardboard, fiberboard, plastic, celluloid, glass, neon tubing, canvas or linen; each has its own value and beauty.

How is it made? Signs used flanges, brackets, arms, stands, and more as a means of display. The more unusual an attachment is, the more desirable the piece will be. Electric or light-up signs need to be in working condition unless you are or have a good electrician.

And lastly and probably most importantly, does it appeal to you? If it is unusual and something that immediately attracted you, then the original artist did his job.

Everyone that enjoys this hobby has their own story of finding a great piece, waiting to buy it, and while thinking it over, that item sold to someone else! Occasionally I am asked, "Where are you going to put that?" This is a question to be pondered only after you have purchased your latest find! As we all know, the time to buy a collectible is when you see it.

I hope you enjoy this compilation of Advertising signs. Each has its own fine qualities and interesting oddities. Browse through these photographs and consider the talent and time it took to produce these advertising collectibles.

AAA/SPRING WATER...
9¾" x 12", porcelain. $100.00(B)

AAA/RECOMMENDED HOTEL
48" x 31½", neon on porcelain (neon missing). $160.00(B)

ABC/IT'S UP TO YOU
13" x 28", framed picture. $110.00(B)

AC/SPARK PLUGS, 5¢ EACH...
Metal. $65.00(D)

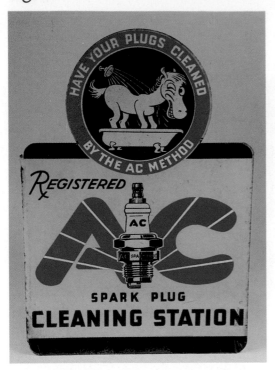

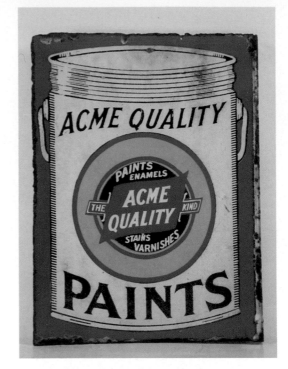

AC/SPARK PLUG CLEANING STATION
1945, 11" x 15½", tin. $140.00(B)

Acme Paints/ACME QUALITY
14½" x 20", porcelain. $55.00(B)

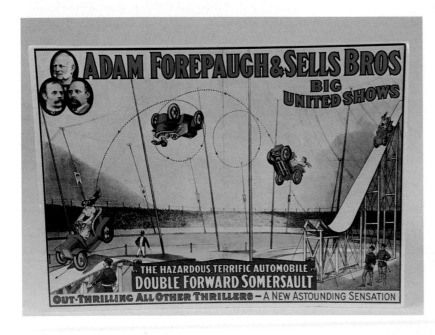

Adam Forepaugh & Sells Bros/CIRCUS
17½" x 13", poster. $50.00(B*)

Aetna/AUTOMOBILE INSURANCE...
24" x 12", tin. $65.00(B)

**Albert F. Wood Manufacturer/
SATIN SKIN POWDER...**
©1903, 28" x 42½", poster. $30.00(B)

**American Motor Hotel Association/
MEMBER 1951**
20" x 25", porcelain. $100.00(B)

American Agriculturist/MEMBER...
1950s, 13½" x 6½". $110.00(B)

**Alliance Coffee/FOR COFFEE
CONTENTMENT SERVE ALLIANCE**
"Pat May 16, 1910," in bottom
corner of picture, 12½" x 16⅛",
die-cut cardboard sign. $225.00(B)

American Express/TRAVELERS CHEQUES...
1930s, 10" x 4½", porcelain. $200.00(B)

**American Negro Exposition/
CHICAGO COLISEUM JULY 4 TO SEPT. 2**
1940, framed 7-color screened print.
$125.00(D)

Amoco/YOUR CAR NEEDS…
37½" x 35", cloth. $85.00(B)

Augustiner/PROPERLY AGED
19⅞" x 13¾", painted tin. $35.00(B)

Atlantic/PURE WHITE LEAD…
20¾" x 35", framed poster. $150.00(B)

Auto-Lite/AUTHORIZED ELECTRIC SERVICE
35¾" x 25½", porcelain. $150.00(B)

B. F. Goodrich/"LITENTUFS"
14" x 19½", cardboard sign. $27.50(D)

Avalon Cigarettes/
YOU'D NEVER GUESS THEY COST YOU LESS
20" x 30", paper on cardboard sign.
$50.00(D)

Baltimore/AMERICAN ALE & BEER...
35¾" x 18", painted tin. $80.00(B)

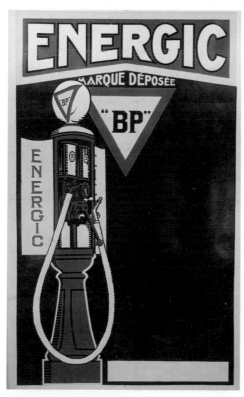

Barns-Dall/
BE SQUARE TO...
3" diameter, pump
sign. $160.00(B)

BP/ENERGIC...
51" x 81". $125.00(B)

**Beacon Shoes/
THERE ARE NO
BETTER...**
14⅜" x 20½",
reverse painted
glass. $70.00(B)

Bickmore/EASY-SHAVE CREAM...
13" x 21", cardboard. $10.00(B)

Beech-nut/CHEWING TOBACCO
22" x 10½", porcelain. $60.00(B)

Betty Rose/COATS & SUITS
24" x 5¼", painted wood sign. $48.00(D)

'blue coal'/CLEAN SAFE LOW COST HEAT
32" x 23½", tin. $55.00(B)

Bell System/PUBLIC TELEPHONE
18" x 18" , flange porcelain. $55.00(B)

Bell System/PUBLIC TELEPHONE
16¼" x 14", flange porcelain. $100.00(B)

Bell System/PUBLIC TELEPHONE
16" x 16", flange porcelain. $350.00(B)

Bell System/PUBLIC TELEPHONE
20" x 20", flange porcelain. $200.00(B)

Bell System/TELEPHONE
19½" x 5¾", metal frame, glass, light-up. $150.00(C)

Blue Crown/GET MORE PEP, SAVE GAS...
14" x 16½", tin. $190.00(B)

Buchanan & Lyall's/PLANET NEPTUNE...
Pat. June 12, 1877, 11½" x 15½", cloth scroll.
$15.00(B)

Borden's/ICE CREAM
24" x 15", painted metal. $300.00(B)

Budweiser Beer/DuBOIS
11" x 9¾", light-up, curved glass front with metal back.
$125.00(B)

Budweiser/CUSTER'S LAST FIGHT
March 30, 1896, 46" x 36", framed lithograph. $275.00(B)

Budweiser/KING OF BEERS
15" x 20", light up sign with convex plastic
cover, old. $100.00(D)

Budweiser Beer/BUDWEISER BEER
10¼" x 8¼", cash register light/sign. $35.00(D)

Butter-Nut/BREAD
Painted metal. $65.00(D)

Buss Auto Fuses/WHY BE HELPLESS...
8½" x 7½", tin. $65.00(B)

CCM/SERVICE STATION-BICYCLES
18" x 10", porcelain. $400.00(B)

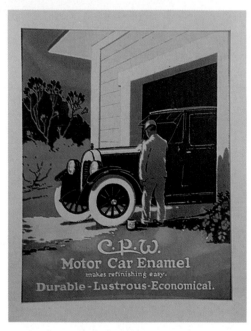

C. P. W./MOTOR CAR ENAMEL...
17¾" x 21¾". $170.00(B)

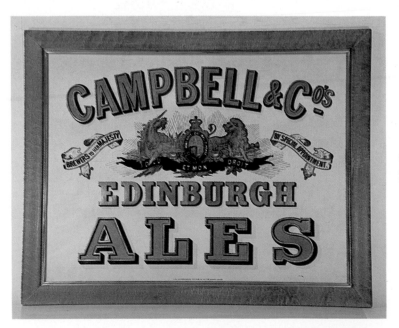

Campbell & Co/EDINBURGH ALES...
28½" x 22⅝". $20.00(B)

Camel/SOLD HERE
Flange porcelain. $75.00(D)

Camel/Prince Albert/
GRAND GIFTS FOR SMOKERS
1946, 10½" x 13¾", paper magazine advertisement. $7.50(D)

Camel/SMOKE CAMEL CIGARETTES
12" x 18", painted metal sign. $42.00(D)

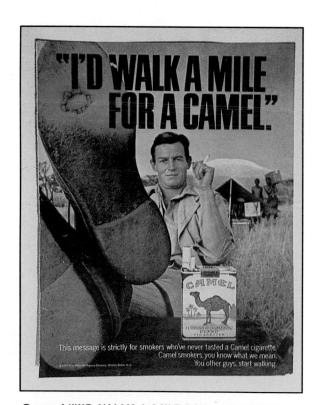

Camel/"I'D WALK A MILE FOR A CAMEL"
8½" x 10¾" x 13¾", paper magazine advertisement. $8.50(D)

"Canada Dry"/COOL OFF...
28" x 34", cardboard. $15.00(B)

Canada Dry/DRINK WINK THE SASSY ONE
26¼" x 16", light-up plastic and metal sign. $50.00(D)

Charmin/
PLEASE DON'T SQUEEZE...
Life-size cardboard cut-out, Mr.
Whipple. $185.00(D)

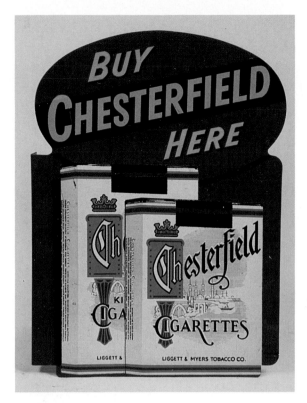

Chesterfield/BUY HERE
11¾" x 16½", painted metal flange.
$30.00(B)

Chesterfield/
BIG CLEAN TASTE OF TOP-TOBACCO
19⅜" x 29¼", tin. $25.00(B)

Chesterfield/BUY CHESTERFIELD HERE
12" x 15", painted metal flange sign.
$38.00(D)

Chesterfield/FULL FLAVORED SATISFACTION
12" x 34", painted tin sign. $40.00(D)

Chrysler Motors/MōPār PARTS...
23¾" x 16¾", metal flange. $185.00(B)

Choctaw/RENTALS SERVICE...
10" x 10", porcelain. $150.00(B)

Cinderella/ICE CREAM
13⅞" x 10⅝", cardboard. $75.00 – $250.00(B*)

**Cochran Paint/
MADE BETTER...**
36" x 24", painted
metal. $25.00(B)

Coca-Cola/SOLD EVERYWHERE
1908, 14" x 22", paper poster. $950.00(B)

Coca-Cola/50TH ANNIVERSARY
1936, 27" x 47", framed poster. $400.00(B)

Coca-Cola/1924 SCENE
1924, right hand side of a two poster scene, left side not shown, 35½" x 20".
$2,500.00(B)

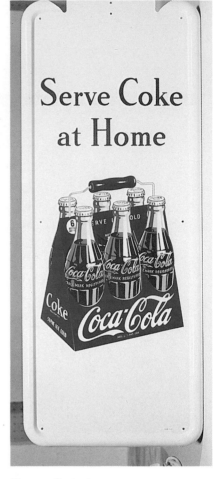

Coca-Cola/
TAKE SOME HOME TODAY
16" x 27", cardboard in
original gold Coca-Cola
issued frame. $575.00(B)

Coca-Cola/DRINK
1930s, die-cut porcelain. $825.00(B)

Coca-Cola/
SERVE COKE AT HOME
NOS, 1947, 16" x 41½". $725.00(B)

Coca-Cola/DRINK ICE COLD
1955, flange. $625.00(B)

Coca-Cola/DRINK
Unusual and rare, 24" iron frame holds
a 16" metal button on one side and a
10" plastic button on the other side.
$825.00(B)

Coca-Cola/HOSPITALITY IN YOUR HANDS
1948, 36" x 20", cardboard. $200.00(B)

Coca-Cola/SOLD HERE ICE COLD
1927, 30" x 21½", arrow with hanging bracket. $650.00(B)

Coca-Cola/WHIRLY BIRD SIGN
NOS, 1950s, eight sided, four winged whirly bird sign. $750.00(B)

Coca-Cola/JOIN THE FRIENDLY CIRCLE
1955, 36" x 20", cardboard. $300.00(B)

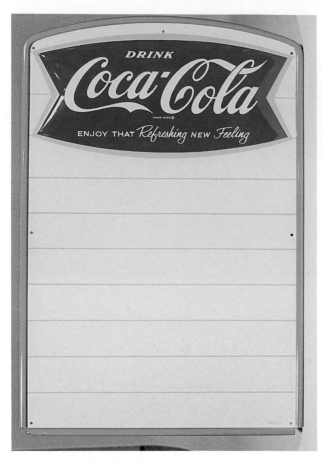

Coca-Cola/REFRESHING NEW FEELING
Menu board, 20" x 30", embossed tin.
$325.00(B)

Coca-Cola/LILLIAN NORDICA
1905, embossed self-framed tin sign. $4,500.00(B)

**Coca-Cola/DRINK COCA-COLA
FOUNTAIN SERVICE**
1939, porcelain. $500.00(B)

**Coca-Cola/
DELICIOUS REFRESHING**
36" x 11½", masonite
and metal. $375.00(B)

Coca-Cola/PLEASE PAY WHEN SERVED
Pressed and raised relief fiberboard. $450.00(B)

Coca-Cola/PLAY REFRESHED
1949, 16" x 27", cardboard poster.
$300.00(B)

**Coca-Cola/RAISED BOTTLE ON
RED BACKGROUND**
NOS, framed metal. $325.00(B)

Coca-Cola/GIRL OFFERING COKE
1926, 11" x 8", tin. $170.00(B)

Coca-Cola/THE PAUSE THAT REFRESHES AT HOME
1941, 56" x 27", framed cardboard advertising. $310.00(B)

**Coca-Cola/BATHING BEAUTY
WITH HAT AND CAPE**
23" x 22", cardboard. $750.00(B)

Coca-Cola/1886 – 1951
Refreshment through the years, festoon. $1,200.00(B)

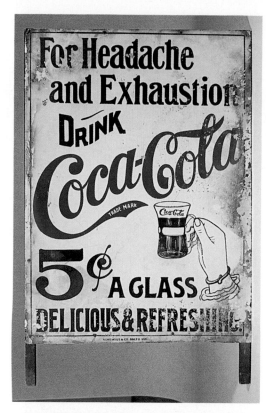

Coca-Cola/HILDA CLARK
1899, 20" x 28", embossed tin. One of three known to exist. Probably the third oldest tin sign for Coca-Cola, first to feature a nationally known star for endorsement. $3,200.00(B)

Coca-Cola/FOR HEADACHE AND EXHAUSTION...
1895–97, 19¾" x 28", with four legs, sidewalk sign manufactured by Ronemous & Co., Baltimore, MD. $6,200.00(B)

Coca-Cola/ON THE REFRESHING SIDE
1941. $575.00(B)

Coca-Cola/WOMAN IN SUIT WITH CARTON OF COKES
1940s, 5' tall, die-cut cardboard. $450.00(B)

Coca-Cola/HOME REFRESHMENT
16" x 27", cardboard. $450.00(B)

Coca-Cola/RECLINING WOMAN
1935, 30" x 50", cardboard. $200.00(B)

Coca-Cola/7 MILLION DRINKS A DAY
18" x 31", cardboard. $1,300.00(B)

Coca-Cola/
JUST A DRINK...BUT WHAT A DRINK
17" x 29¾", cardboard. $180.00(B)

Coca-Cola/ICE COLD...
Painted metal. $245.00(B)

Coca-Cola/
COKE BOTTLE
1930s, 3-dimensional
bottle on painted
metal. $350.00(D)

Coca-Cola/
SCHOOL CROSSING GUARD
Metal on round metal base.
$1,000.00(D)

Coca-Cola/COKE BATHING GIRL
18" x 28", die-cut cardboard. $1,400.00(B)

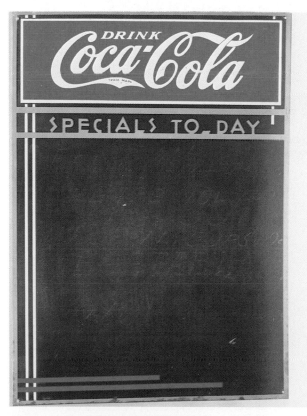

Coca-Cola/SPECIALS TO-DAY
1930s, menu board. $150.00(B)

**Continental Trailways/
BUS DEPOT**
36" x 18", porcelain. $125.00(B)

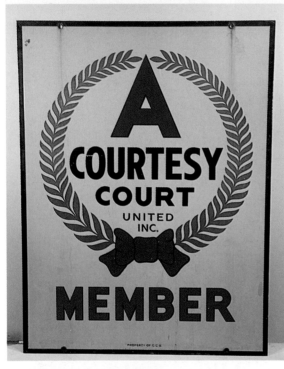

Courtesy Court/MEMBER...
36" x 48", porcelain. $25.00(B)

**Crazy Water Crystals/
JUST ADD IT TO YOUR DRINKING WATER**
9¾" x 13½", cardboard sign with attached
cardboard easel. $45.00(D)

Crosley/RADIOS AND HOME APPLIANCES
Neon. $475.00(D)

The Crystal Flash Line/JUST A LITTLE BETTER
99" x 47", die cut porcelain. $850.00(B)

Dairy Brand/ONE OF AMERICA'S FINEST DAIRIES...
Framed glass light-up. $225.00(C)

Defense Bonds/SANTA
24" x 30", framed poster. $60.00(B)

Dairy Brand/ENJOY DAIRY BRAND MILK–ICE CREAM
Reflective metal. $65.00(C)

Dairy Brand/MILK–ICE CREAM
25¾" x 6¾", metal framed glass light-up. $300.00(C)

Dee-Light/DRINK DEE-LIGHT, IT'S DEE-LICIOUS
6" x 17¾". $5.00(B)

De Laval/WE USE...
Painted metal. $65.00(D)

Delco-light/DEPENDABLE...
19½" x 9", painted metal. $10.00(B)

Delco/BATTERY SERVICE...
30" x 22", tin. $160.00(B)

**DeNobili Cigar Company/
PALM CIGARS**
19" x 6", embossed tin. $15.00(B)

**Dixie Oil Co./
DIXIE...**
1970s, porcelain
gas pump sign.
$170.00(B)

**Department of Health/
'SPITTING ON SIDEWALKS...**
10" x 7", tin. $90.00(B)

Dr Pepper/5¢ GAS...
Blackboard and tin. $850.00(B)

**Dr Pepper/
HAVE A PICNIC...**
New York World's Fair
poster. $21.00(D)

F. F. Lewis/SAILOR BOY
5¾" x 8½", die-cut cardboard.
$25.00(B)

Dr Pepper/GOOD FOR LIFE!...
26½" x 10½", porcelain. $180.00(B)

Duquesne Pilsener/DUQUESNE PILSENER
24½" x 6", metal framed glass, light-up. $85.00(B)

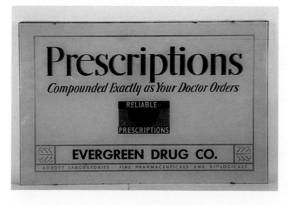

**Evergreen Drug Co./
PRESCRIPTIONS...**
18" x 12", reverse
painted glass.
$40.00(B)

Esso/PUT A TIGER IN YOUR TANK
42" x 83", plastic banner.
$110.00(B)

Falstaff/ENJOY FALSTAFF BEER
17½" x 15", painted metal 2-piece sign.
$95.00(D)

Falstaff/AN OLD FRIEND
17½" x 15", painted metal sign. $95.00(D)

Falstaff/AMERICA'S PREMIUM QUALITY BEER/Falstaff symbol
13½" x 18", revolving plastic topped sign.
$125.00(D)

Falstaff/AMERICA'S PREMIUM QUALITY BEER
10¾" x 26", Gene Pressler girl print (repro) in painted glass and metal frame. $210.00(D)

Fatima/ TURKISH CIGARETTES
© 1909 by S. Anargyos, NY. 27" x 36½", sign in original frame. $175.00(B)

Feen-a-mint/ FOR CONSTIPATION...
29¼" x 7", porcelain.
$55.00(B)

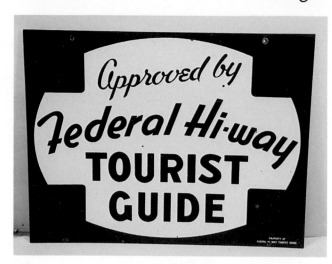

Federal Hi-Way/TOURIST GUIDE
30" x 24", porcelain. $30.00(B)

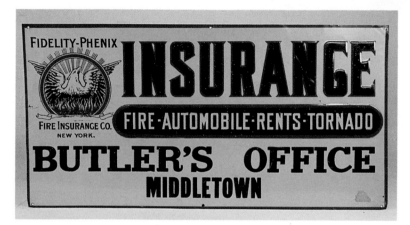

Fidelity-Phenix/INSURANCE
23¼" x 11¾", tin. $80.00(B)

Fisk/RED TOPS...
12½" x 17", print. $70.00(B)

Firestone/CYCLE TIRES...
22" x 11½", metal. $300.00(B)

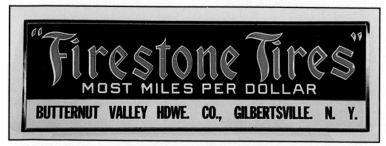

"Firestone Tires"/MOST MILES PER DOLLAR...
35½" x 11½", tin. $100.00(B)

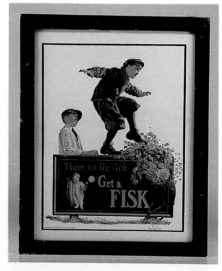

Fisk/TIME TO RE-TIRE...
11" x 14", framed print. $50.00(B)

Ford/FORD
70" x 35½", tin, light-up. $1,450.00(B)

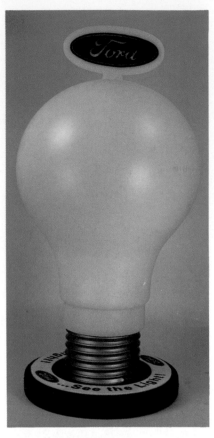

Ford/SEE THE LIGHT
1960s, 11" x 26" advertising light
bulb. $110.00(B)

Fordor/SEDAN
1928, 34½" x 24", poster. $130.00(B)

Fred'K Gamash/AUTOMOBILES...
19¾" x 13⅝". $145.00(B)

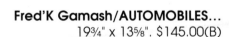

Francisco/AUTO HEATER
40" x 18", self contained
framed tin. $425.00(B)

French/WINE COCA 5¢
1885–1888, 27¾" x 19¾", embossed tin. $5,700.00(B)

Close-up of the French Wine Coca tin.

Friedman Co./ROYALTY CLUB WHISKEY...
31" x 21", framed painted glass. $80.00(B)

Fruit Bowl/DRINK...
18½" x 14". $50.00(B)

**Gillette Tires/
A BEAR FOR WEAR**
72½" x 19¼", tin. $50.00(B)

Goodrich Tires/AIR SERVICE
11" x 9", porcelain. $110.00(B)

Goodrich/HOT WATER HEATER...
57" x 34", paper. $10.00(B)

**Goodrich/BATTERIES•
TIRES • ACCESSORIES**
60" x 20½", porcelain.
$100.00(B)

Goodyear/TIRES...
$75.00(D)

Goodyear/TIRE AND BATTERY SERVICE
Embossed painted metal. $55.00(D)

Grape-Nuts/TO SCHOOL WELL FED...
20¼" x 30¼", self-contained tin sign.
$1,100.00(B)

Goodyear/GOODYEAR TIRES
25" x 8", framed light-up. $55.00(B)

Grapette/ENJOY...
Oval painted metal. $175.00(D)

Googh's/SARSAPARILLA...
11" x 14", framed paper. $110.00(B)

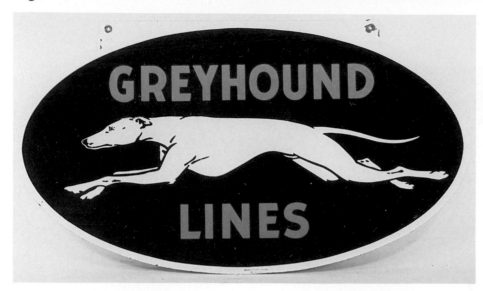

**Greyhound/
GREYHOUND LINES**
36" x 20½", porcelain. $200.00 –
$300.00(B*)

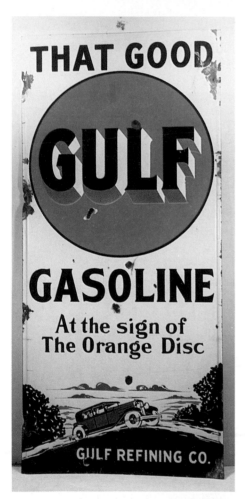

Gulf/GULF
Round plastic light-up. $150.00(D)

Gulf/THAT GOOD GASOLINE...
27½" x 60", porcelain. $440.00(B)

Gulf/GULF
Plastic letters on
metal strips.
$95.00(D)

Hamm's Beer/BORN IN THE LAND OF SKY BLUE WATERS
31" x 18", plastic light-up, moving landscape photograph. $200.00(C)

Hamilton, Brown/SHOES
19½" x 14", painted metal flange. $25.00(B)

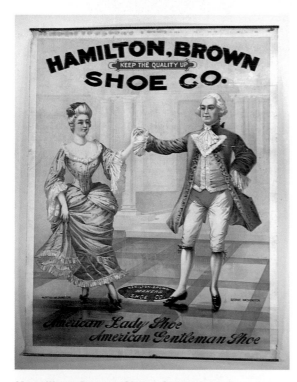

Hamilton, Brown Shoe Company/ KEEP THE QUALITY...
29¾" x 39¾", paper. $210.00(B)

Helmar/TURKISH CIGARETTES
3⅝" x 21⅝", cardboard on wood. $5.00(B)

Hershey's/ICE CREAM
Painted metal. $105.00(D)

Hires/IN BOTTLES...
27" x 10", tin. $85.00(B)

Hoffman's/FIRST CHOICE ICE CREAM
25¾" x 22", porcelain with arm. $140.00(B)

Hollywood Glow/SKIN TONIC
Cardboard sign. $35.00(D)

Honest Tobacco/MAN IN HAT
Late nineteenth century, cardboard in frame. $750.00 – $2,000.00(B*)

Hudson-Rambler/SALES SERVICE
42" x 30", porcelain. $475.00(B)

Illinois Valley/ICE CREAM
Plastic, light-up. $145.00(D)

Illinois Watch Company/FACTORY
24⅝" x 16½", print in frame. $50.00(B)

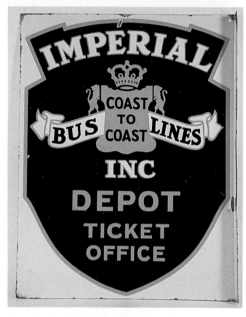

Imperial Bus Lines/DEPOT...
18" x 24", flange porcelain.
$450.00(B)

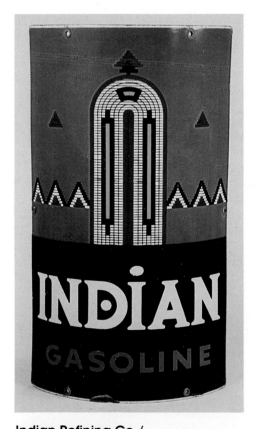

**Indian Refining Co./
INDIAN GASOLINE...**
12" x 18", porcelain. $155.00(B)

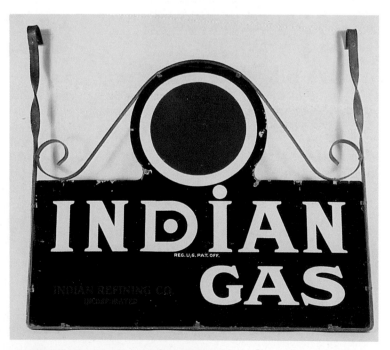

Indian Refining Co./INDIAN GAS...
45" x 36", porcelain. $500.00(B)

Interwoven Socks/
NORMAN ROCKWELL ILLUSTRATION
28" x 38", paper-linen. $80.00(B)

J. P. Coats/SPOOL COTTON
18" x 30", hard-board on wooden frame.
$300.00(B)

Jeep/WILLYS SALES & SERVICE…
25" x 27", porcelain. $80.00(B)

John Deere/FARM IMPLEMENTS
72" x 23¾", porcelain, double sided sign. $875.00(B)

John Dewar & Sons/OLD WORLD SCENE
31¼" x 22¼", cardboard in original oak
frame. $10.00(B)

Johnson & Johnson/FOR BABIES…
14½" x 22", cardboard. $80.00(B)

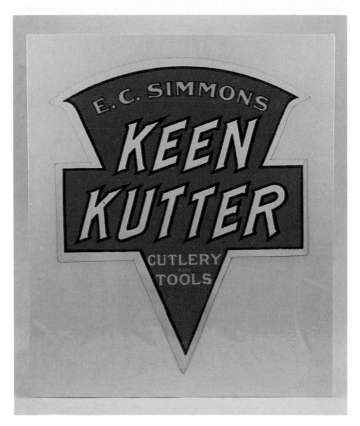

Keen Kutter/CUTLERY AND TOOLS
10¼" x 13", cardboard. $30.00(B)

Keen Kutter/ALWAYS READY TO SHAVE…
20¾" x 10¾", cardboard. $30.00(B)

Keen Kutter/H. C. STALLIONS HDW. CO.
Embossed painted metal. $175.00(C)

Kendall Oil Company/THE DEALER SIGN OF QUALITY
Embossed painted metal.
$85.00(D)

Kelly Tires/KELLY TIRES...
24" diameter, metal flange. $1,250.00 – $4,000.00(B)

Keystone/ICE CREAM
28" x 20", porcelain with arm. $140.00(B)

Kirkman's/THE HANDY SHAPE...
21" x 11", trolley car sign. $130.00(B)

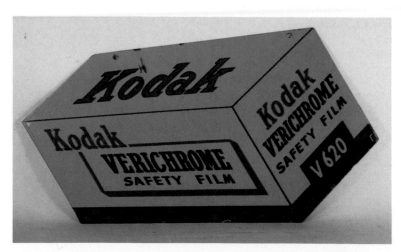

Kodak/VERICHROME
24½" x 12½", porcelain. $200.00(B)

Kool Cigarettes/WE SELL CIGARETTES
25" x 10½", embossed painted tin. $54.00(D)

Kool Cigarettes/
GIRL WITH MASK AND SCARF
32" x 47", framed die cut cardboard. $150.00(B)

Ladies Home Journal/IRENE BORDONI
46" x 34", framed cloth banner. $300.00(B)

Lee Tires/LEE TIRES
32" x 7½", metal framed
light-up. $135.00(B)

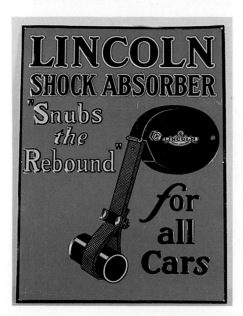

Lincoln/SHOCK
ABSORBER...
17½" x 24", tin.
$180.00(B)

Lions/
INTERNATIONAL
30" diameter,
porcelain.
$100.00(B)

Litchfield/ICE CREAM
Metal framed plastic light-up. $135.00(D)

Little Giant Farm Equipment/ELEVATORS
Painted metal. $65.00(D)

Lohrey's/AT YOUR SERVICE
13" x 19", framed painted glass. $50.00(B)

Lucky Strike/HARRY HEILMANN
21" x 11", framed trolley card. $1,100.00(B)

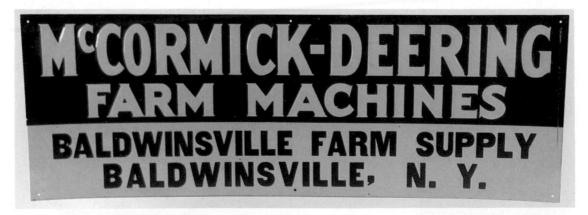

McCormick–Deering/FARM MACHINES
27½" x 10", painted tin. $75.00(B)

M H & M Shoes/ARM AND HAND
28" x 6½", embossed tin. $220.00(B)

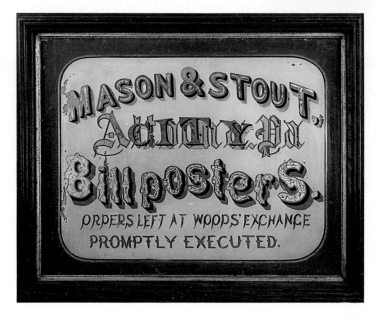

Mason & Stout/BILL POSTERS...
23½" x 19½", wooden framed, reverse painted glass. $100.00(B)

Massachusetts Highway Commission/CORNER...
24¼" x 16", porcelain. $300.00(B)

Masury/PAINTS–VARNISHES...
36" x 24". $25.00(B)

**Melachrino/
THE ONE CIGARETTE...**
28" x 4", cardboard
with wooden frame.
$30.00(B)

Millers Falls/THE SAFEST NAME IN TOOLS
Metal framed, plastic light-up. $45.00(C)

Melox/DOG FOODS
18" x 26", porcelain sign.
$750.00(B)

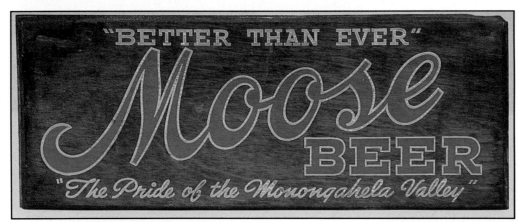

**Moose Beer/
"BETTER THAN EVER..."**
15" x 6⅞", wooden.
$85.00(B)

Moosehead/ON TAP...
Neon. $175.00(B)

Motorola/CAR RADIO...
$125.00(D)

Mobil Oil/PEGASUS
3' tall, porcelain. $450.00(B)

Mobilgas/FRANK NESS
10" x 8", framed photo. $30.00(B)

Mobilgas/MOBILGAS SPECIAL
1947, 12" x 12", porcelain pump sign.
$100.00(B)

Mobiloil/CERTIFIED SERVICE...
19½" square, porcelain. $375.00(B)

Nash/AUTHORIZED SERVICE...
42" x 42", porcelain. $480.00(B)

Neuweiler's Beer/
WATCH THE PLACE A WHILE, JOE...
17¼" x 13¾", cardboard sign. $55.00(D)

National Automobile Club/SAFETY FIRST...
30" x 27", porcelain. $240.00(B)

National Distillers/NOTICE...
22" x 14", porcelain. $280.00(B)

Navy/GEE I WISH I WERE A MAN...
25" x 49", Howard Chandler Christy
poster. $300.00(B)

Navy/I WANT YOU...
1917, 26½" x 41", World War I cloth
backed poster signed by Howard Chandler Christy. $100.00(B)

Nehi/DRINK NEHI
45" x 18", painted tin. $75.00(B)

Navy/SIX MILLION CHEERS
20" x 29", poster. $60.00(B)

New Era/ICE CREAM
24¾" x 14¾", neon. $350.00(C)

Niagara/DRINK NIAGARA PUNCH
9" x 20", tin. $100.00(B)

No Company/USED CARS...
36" diameter, porcelain. $230.00(B)

**No Company/
5¢ A DANCE**
Neon (new).
$200.00(B)

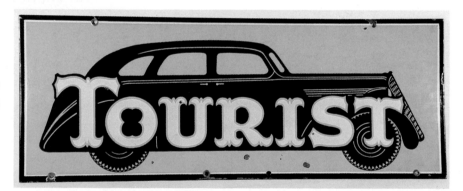

No Company/TOURIST
35" x 13", porcelain. $1,000.00(B)

**No Company/
COOL AND COMFORTABLE INSIDE**
62" x 15½", wooden. $75.00(B)

No Company/WILSON NEEDS...
37½" x 12", porcelain. $75.00(B)

No Company/SERVICE...
59¼" x 9½", porcelain. $250.00(B)

Nugrape/MORE FUN WITH...
Round painted metal.
$95.00(D)

No Company/WOMEN'S ROOM
1939, 12" x 13", porcelain. $160.00(B)

Nutmeg/ICE COLD CLUB BEVERAGES...
28" x 10", tin. $95.00(B)

Oilzum/BARTER'S GARAGE
60" x 36", two sided tin.
$1,700.00(B)

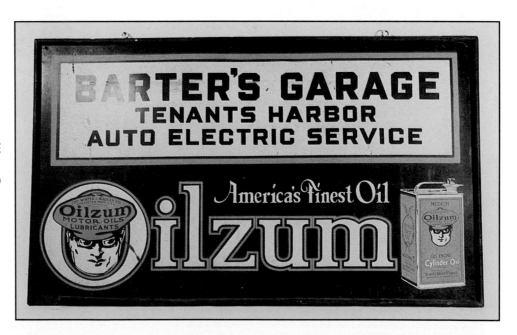

Old Gold/NOT A COUGH...
36" x 11", porcelain. $200.00(B)

Old Gold/CIGARETTES
36" x 12", porcelain. $5.00(B)

Old Overholt Whiskey/FISHERMAN...
1913, 27½" x 38½", oleograph canvas
in wood frame. $300.00(B*)

Old Reliable Coffee/
WELCOME AS APRIL SHOWERS...
21" x 11", trolley car sign. $150.00(B)

Old Style/BREWED WITH WATER FROM
WHEN THE EARTH WAS PURE
15" x 10¼", light up plastic sign. $15.00(D)

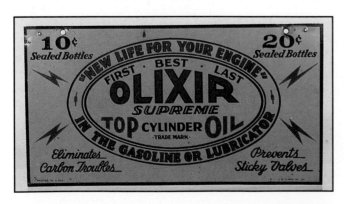

Olixir/"NEW LIFE FOR YOUR ENGINE..."
16" x 9", metal. $25.00(B)

Oliver/IMPLEMENTS
18" x 18", flange tin. $160.00(B)

Opex/HEADQUARTERS
22" x 16", flange porcelain. $200.00(B)

Overland Co./STOP AT...
25" x 13", tin. $200.00(B)

Pabst Blue Ribbon/
AT POPULAR PRICES
26" x 60", painted tin. $75.00(B)

Overland/SERVICE...
23½" x 12", tin. $150.00(B)

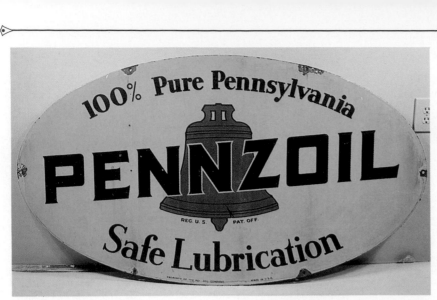

Pennzoil/100% PURE
62" x 35", porcelain. $20.00(B)

Phillips 66/PHILLIPS 66 SHIELD
29" x 29", embossed porcelain. $145.00(B)

**Pennzoil/
SOUND YOUR Z**
Painted metal.
$95.00(D)

Pepto-Bismol/CUT OUT BOTTLE
10⅞" x 27¼", cardboard. $45.00(B)

Peter Schuyler/CIGAR
36" x 12", porcelain. $100.00(B)

Pepsi-Cola/(2-SIDED) BE SOCIABLE
36" x 24¾", cardboard. $95.00(C)

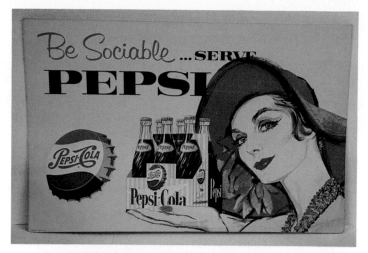

Pepsi-Cola/DRINK...
Tin. $95.00(D)

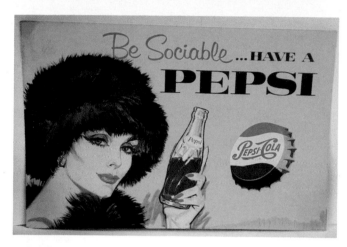

Pepsi-Cola/DRINK PEPSI-COLA
58½" x 36", embossed tin. $120.00(B)

Pepsi-Cola/MORE BOUNCE
36" x 14", tin. $180.00(B)

Phinney-Walker/
CLOCKS FOR AUTOMOBILES...
15" x 20", cardboard. $375.00(B)

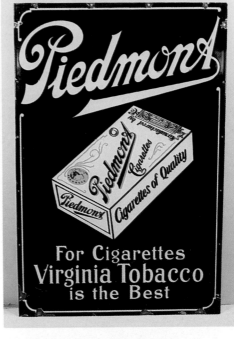

Piedmont/FOR CIGARETTES
VIRGINIA TOBACCO IS THE BEST
30" x 49", porcelain. $100.00(B)

Pittsburgh Brewing/
FROM PITTSBURGH BREWING CO.
40½" x 22", cardboard. $55.00(B)

Poll-Parrot/
SHOES FOR BOYS — FOR GIRLS
Die-cut sidewalk sign, 2-sided.
$1,000.00(B)

Poll-Parrot/BIRD
22" x 38", neon over porcelain sign. $1,150.00(B)

Pontiac/AUTHORIZED SERVICE
41½" diameter, porcelain. $225.00(B)

Post Toasties/WITH PEACHES AND CREAM...
15¼" x 12¼", paper. $110.00(B)

Popsicle/EVERYBODY LIKES...
28" x 10", tin. $375.00(B)

Quadriga Cloth/THE GIRL WHO SEWS HAS BETTER CLOTHES
20" x 6½", cut out wooden sign. $55.00(D)

Quick Meal/CHICK & EGG...
44¾" x 33½", porcelain. $185.00(B)

Quaker State/
MOTOR OIL CERTIFIED GUARANTEED
26½" x 29", porcelain. $70.00(B)

Quaker State/35¢ PER QUART
13¾" x 9¾", embossed metal. $50.00(B)

Randolph Hotel/J. S. R.
15¼" diameter, mirror. $35.00(B)

Red Crown Gasoline/CROWN IN THE CENTER
42" diameter, circular porcelain. $800.00(B)

Remer's/TEA STORE
10" x 6¼", cardboard. $25.00(B)

**Red Goose Shoes/
FIGURAL GOOSE**
Neon outlined goose
(reproduction). $350.00(C)

Redmen Archery/SHOOT
24" x 34", wood. $350.00 - $700.00(B*)

Red Seal/DRY BATTERY
Flanged metal. $100.00(D)

Robert Bosch/PYRO-ACTION...
19¾" x 12¼", tin. $110.00(B)

Richfield/HERE SOON
39½" x 54½", poster. $175.00(B)

SWP/COVER THE EARTH…
48" x 36", porcelain. $70.00(B)

Royal/INSURANCE COMPANY LIMITED
22¼" x 31¼", wooden. $80.00(B)

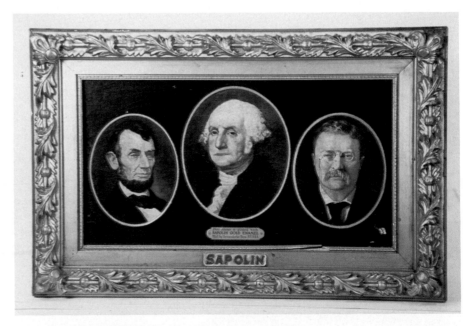

Sapolin/THREE PRESIDENTS
21" x 13½", framed advertising marked: "This frame is gilded with sapolin gold enamel MFD by Gerstendorfer Bros. NY, USA." $65.00(B)

Royal Crown Cola/BOTTLE
15¾" x 59¾", painted metal. $130.00(B)

**Sealy Mattress/
COTTON FIELD SCENE**
61" x 41", cardboard. $110.00(B)

Sealtest/ROSZELL'S
Neon. $175.00(D)

Sealtest/ICE CREAM
35¾" x 23⅞". $25.00(B)

Seven-up/OPEN...
Painted metal. $45.00(D)

Sinclair/PENNSYLVANIA MOTOR OIL...
11" diameter, porcelain pump sign.
$250.00(B)

Southern Cowley/DANGER SOUND KLAXON
24¾" x 18¾", wooden. $100.00(B)

Sparrow's Chocolates/LITTLE GIRL ON TABLE
17" x 24¼", tin. $300.00(B)

Squeeze/DRINK…
28" x 20", tin. $140.00(B)

**Standard Oil Company/
PERFECTION KEROSENE**
18" x 14", flange tin. $110.00(B)

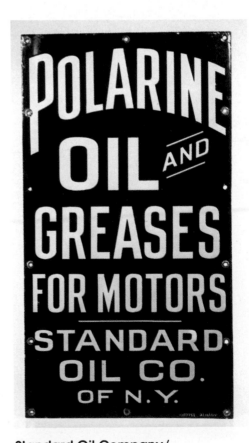

**Standard Oil Company/
POLARINE OIL…**
12" x 22", porcelain. $300.00(B)

Standard Oil Co./SOCONY AIR-CRAFT OILS...
30" x 20", porcelain. $350.00(B)

**Standard Oil Co./
SOCONY MOTOR OIL...**
8" x 9½", porcelain. $600.00(B)

Stoeckers/IT'S GOT THE PEP...
$45.00(D)

Sun Spot/BOTTLED SUNSHINE
Flange. $175.00(D)

**Sweet-Orr/
PANTS, OVERALLS, SHIRTS...**
24" x 10", porcelain.
$200.00(B)

Sylvania/HALO LIGHT
20" x 19", neon sign. $250.00(D)

Texaco/SKY CHIEF SU-PREME...
12" x 18", porcelain. $40.00(B)

Texaco/TEXACO MOTOR OIL
16" x 22", flange porcelain. $500.00(B)

Tube Rose/SNUFF
27⅝" x 17½", painted tin. $85.00(B)

Tydol/FLYING A...
9¾" diameter. $170.00(B)

Tydol/THE LUBRICATION GASOLINE...
14" x 9¾", metal. $175.00(B)

Tydol/FILL UP WITH...
79" x 34", cloth banner. $155.00(B)

U. S. Army/I WANT YOU
33" x 43", framed James Montgomery
Flag poster. $250.00(B)

U. S. Government/SMOKEY BEAR
12½" x 18", It's A Grand Old Forest Too.
Be Careful, framed poster. $100.00(C)

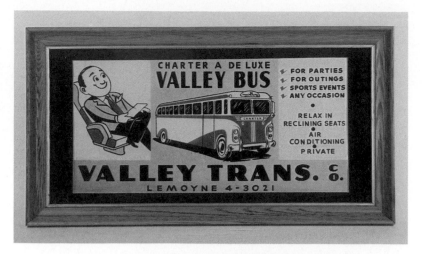

Union 76/CERTIFIED...
22" diameter, porcelain. $190.00(B)

Valley Transportation Company/CHARTER A DE LUXE...
26¼" x 14¼". $30.00(B)

Viceroy/OPEN
15¾" x 9", plastic sign. $9.00(D)

Van Houten's/COCOA
24¼" x 30¼", cardboard in original oak frame, (frame etched Van Houten's Coca). $30.00(B)

Veedol/TIME TO CHANGE TO...
58" x 36", cloth banner. $120.00(B)

Velvet/AMERICA'S SMOOTHEST SMOKE
39" x 12", porcelain. $35.00(B)

Ward's Orange Crush/DRINK...
28" x 20", tin. $110.00(B)

Welch/DRINK A BUNCH OF GRAPES...
40" x 18", tin. $450.00(B)

**Western Union/TELEPHONE
YOUR TELEGRAMS FROM HERE**
18" x 19½", flanged porcelain
sign. $75.00(B)

White Rose/FLOUR BAKES BETTER BREAD
74" x 26", wooden. $275.00(B)

Whitman's/CHOCOLATES
39½" x 13½", porcelain. $120.00(B)

Willys-Overland Co./WHIPPET...
36" x 24", porcelain. $300.00(B)

Will's Cigarettes/W. D. & H. O. WILLS...
13" x 24", framed sign. $150.00(B)

Wolf's Head/WE SELL…
59" diameter curb sign, cast base
with raised letters. $290.00(B)

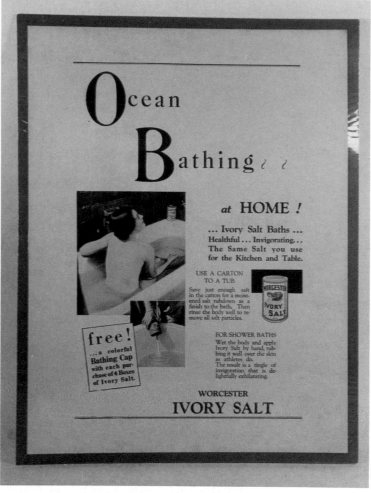

Worcester/OCEAN BATHING AT HOME…
14" x 19", paper. $10.00(B)

Zero Flo/
POURS AT 35˚ BELOW…
28" x 20", tin. $140.00(B)

CLOCKS

We have the ideal night-light in our house. It is an old light-up Sealtest Ice-Cream advertising clock. It looks great and is always a conversation starter. Advertising clocks present a wonderful and ingenious format for manufacturers to keep their product in view and on the customer's mind constantly. They serve as a subliminal message to buy their product each time you glance at the time of day! Clocks may be lighted from behind with the face glowing, or flooded with light on its face from the sides. Often they include a larger area just for advertising the product with the clock setting to the side, above, or below. Because moving parts are inherent to a clock, often the art styles include moving parts to draw the customers attention. These advertising pieces may be driven by several means. Weights and chains are a form that must be periodically adjusted as must spring clocks. Electricity is a most popular means because there is no regular maintenance involved and lights can be employed to draw attention. Since I am not a mechanical wizard, I try to make certain the clock mechanism works. The lighting features are not as difficult to repair, but the time-keeping works will almost certainly need a professional if they are not in proper working order. Lighting is an interesting feature with these pieces. Incandescent bulbs are often used because of their availability. Florescent lighting was developed in the 1930s and came into public use in 1938. Good light-up clocks can still be found for under $100.00. Neon lighting, generated in glass tubing when the gas inside is exposed to an electric current, is a favorite of mine. Pure neon gas reacts to an electric discharge with a brilliant red color and other colors are produced by introducing more and varied gases. Neon lighting also has the ability to pierce heavy fog so it is used extensively out-of-doors. Some advertising clocks have employed neon as an artful added bonus. Neons will command $300.00 and more depending on the design. Neons can be repaired or charged in my area for about $45.00 a unit. So if the clock face is good and the neon broken, it still can be salvaged. The prices on light-up clocks of all kinds seem to have risen rapidly over the past few years, so if you want one, now is the time. Collecting these time pieces has only one major draw-back and that is power failure! Living in the country, this happens often and when these failures occur, re-setting these collectibles can be tedious!

**American-Standard/
HEATING-AIR CONDITIONING**
Light-up clock. $135.00(C)

Budweiser/DU BOISE
Light-up clock. $200.00(B)

Cadillac/SERVICE
Clock. $165.00(D)

Chappell's/MILK
Light-up clock. $125.00(C)

Coca-Cola/IN BOTTLES
1930s, Gilbert pendulum clock.
$1,000.00(B)

Coca-Cola/REGULATOR
1905, Ingraham clock. $900.00(B)

Coca-Cola/DRINK COCA COLA IN BOTTLES
1939-40, 16" x 16", wood framed clock. $160.00(B)

Coca-Cola/ROUND
Reproduction clock. $275.00(D)

Coca-Cola/RX
Neon reproduction. $225.00(D)

Coca-Cola/BOTTLE SHAPED
1910, 3" x 8", leather boudoir
clock. $750.00(B)

Delaware Punch/DELICIOUS ANYTIME
Clock. $145.00(D)

Duquesne Brewing Company/DUKE BEER
Light-up clock. $30.00(B)

Elgin/ARTHUR J. NYMAN
Light-up clock. $350.00(D)

FTD/INTERFLORA• WORLDWIDE
Light-up clock. $120.00(D)

Griesedieck Bros./IT'S DE-BITTERIZED
Round, metal framed clock. $135.00(D)

Firestone/TIRES-BATTERIES
15¼" x 15¼", clock. $100.00(B)

Gruen/WATCH TIME
Light-up clock. $385.00(D)

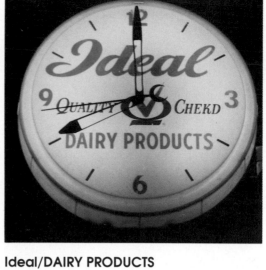

Ideal/DAIRY PRODUCTS
15½" diameter, light-up clock.
$135.00(C)

Independent/CIRCULAR
Light-up clock. $65.00(D)

Mobil/SERVICE
Clock. $145.00(D)

Monroe/AMERICA RIDES
Light-up clock. $97.00(D)

Neon Clock Sales Co./THANK YOU CALL AGAIN
Square, neon clock. $350.00(D)

NuGrape/
IF YOU ONLY KNEW WHAT GOES INTO...
Light-up clock. $225.00(D)

NuGrape/SQUARE
13¼" x 16", light-up clock. $125.00(C)

New Era Dairy/VELVET RICH ICE CREAM
24¾" x 11¾", light-up clock. $250.00(C)

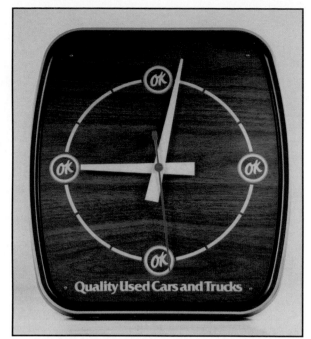

OK/QUALITY USED CARS
13" x 15", clock. $20.00(B)

Oilzum/CHOICE OF CHAMPIONS
14½" diameter, light-up clock. $950.00(B)

Oilzum/CHOICE OF CHAMPIONS
16" square clock. $160.00(B)

Orange Crush/TASTE
Light-up clock. $95.00(C)

Pennsylvania/MOTOR OIL
15" diameter, light-up clock. $230.00(B)

Prairie Farms/MILK, ICE CREAM
16" diameter, plastic clock. $75.00(C)

Quaker State/MOTOR OIL
Light-up clock. $300.00(D)

Red Goose/CIRCULAR
Light-up clock. $550.00(B)

Rexall/COMPARE THE PRICE…
Light-up clock. $65.00(D)

S & H Green Stamps/WE GIVE...
15¼" x 22¾", light-up clock. $75.00(B)

Sealtest/DAIRY PRODUCTS
15¼" square, light-up clock. $95.00(C)

Studebaker/BATTERIES
15¼" square, light-up clock. $115.00(B)

Swift's/ICE CREAM
Light-up clock. $75.00(D)

Texaco/MANSFIELD TIRES
Light-up clock. $175.00(D)

Timley Clothes/MINUTEMAN WITH BELL
18" x 18½", plastic and metal clock. $125.00(D)

**United Van Lines/
W. JEFF HAMMOND**
Light-up clock. $140.00(D)

Vanderbilt/PREMIUM TIRES
1958, 14½" diameter, light-up clock. $120.00(B)

Velvet/ICE CREAM
Light-up clock. $195.00(D)

Velvet/ICE CREAM AND DAIRY PRODUCTS
15½" square, light-up clock. $150.00(C)

Velvet/MILK & ICE CREAM
Light-up clock. $45.00(D)

Vess/BILLION BUBBLE BEVERAGES
Light-up clock. $125.00(D)

Wolf's Head/MOTOR OIL & LUBES
Round clock. $325.00(D)

Wynn's/FRICTION PROOFING
Clock. $95.00(D)

CALENDARS

A natural time-charting extension beyond clocks is the calendar. This advertising item would keep a product in view 365 days a year, and as a result mountains of calendars have been produced by manufacturers over the years. Some calendars use a single advertising piece with tear off calendar pads for the whole year, while others have different ads for each month. Seasons would often influence the art used for this form of advertising. Phases of the moon can also be chronicled along with special holidays or historical events. Another wonderful feature presented by these pieces is the proliferation of art work by famous artists that the general public might not have otherwise had the chance to enjoy. An entire advertising genre has been generated by advertising calendars and has even influenced the calendar manufacturing market of today.

Bayerson/OIL WORKS
1914 calendar. $50.00(B)

Chevrolet/MOTOR CARS
1920 calendar. $145.00(B)

Coca-Cola/GIRL WITH SNOW SKIES
1947 calendar. $140.00(B)

Coca-Cola/A MOMENT ON THE SUNNYSIDE
1944 calendar. $300.00(B)

Coca-Cola/FREEMONT PHARMACY
1928 framed calendar. $750.00(B)

Coca-Cola/ELAINE
1915 framed calendar. $3,600.00(B)

Coca-Cola/BLUE GIRL WITH HAT
1921 framed calendar. $850.00(B)

Coca-Cola/FLAPPER
1929 framed calendar. $210.00(B)

Coca-Cola/VICTORIAN GIRL AT TABLE
1898 framed calendar remnant. $550.00(B)

Coca-Cola/WOMEN AT BEACH
1918 framed calendar top.
$900.00(B)

Coca-Cola/SODA FOUNTAIN
1901 calendar. $1,350.00(B)

Coca-Cola/BETTY
1914 calendar. $1,600.00(B)

Coca-Cola/U. S. ARMY NURSE CORPS
1943 calendar. $425.00(B)

Coca-Cola/JUNE CAPRICE
1918 framed calendar. $250.00(B)

Coca-Cola/BOY AT WELL
1932 framed calendar. $625.00(B)

Collins Baking Co./COLLINS CELEBRATED BREAD
1909, 8" x 8" calendar. $25.00(B)

**Dr Pepper/THE FRIENDLY PEPPER UPPER-
GIRL IN BOWLING ALLEY**
1961, 16" x 23½" calendar. $25.00(D)

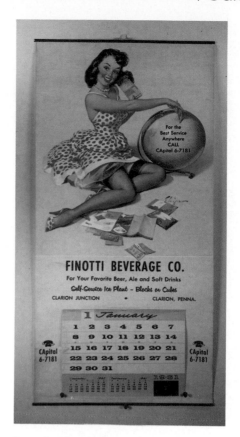

**Finotti Beverage Co./
GIRL WITH GLOBE**
1961 calendar. $25.00(B)

H.S. Eshleman/AUTO REPAIRING
1928 calendar. $175.00(B)

L.E. Graybill/HOTEL & RESTAURANT
1923, 15" x 15", 3-dimensional calendar. $12.00(D)

**Missouri Pacific Lines/
TRAIN ENGINE ON TRACKS**
Calendar. $85.00(B)

Mobiloil/MAGNOLIA TRAIL
1933 calendar. $75.00(B)

No Company/WINTER SCENE
1911, oval, German calendar. $50.00(B)

Slicker Pipe and Tool Company/
OIL AND GAS WELL SUPPLIES
1927 calendar. $30.00(B)

Slicker Pipe & Tool Co./
BOYS IN SWIMMING HOLE
1926 calendar. $30.00(B)

Socony/
GAS PUMP AND ATTENDANT
Calendar top. $90.00(B)

Texaco/
PETROLEUM AND ITS PRODUCTS
1922 calendar. $185.00(B)

Pennsylvania Railroad/MASS TRANSPORTATION
1955 calendar. $45.00(B)

Pennsylvania Railroad/VITAL LINES TO WORLD TRADE
1957 calendar. $30.00(B)

Pennsylvania Railroad/CONWAY YARD
1958 calendar. $30.00(B)

Pennsylvania Railroad/DYNAMIC PROGRESS
1956 calendar. $10.00(B)

THERMOMETERS

Although my memory seems to compare with the attention span of your average teen-ager, I still remember the first advertising thermometer I acquired. I use the word acquire because stole has such a negative and illegal ring to it. Every family has at least one "real character" in it. Ours is my wife's Uncle Ed, a collector of great "stuff." Well, Ed and I decided one day to check out the remains of a building that a friend of his was tearing down. As soon as we pulled into the field where the old building was laying in ruins I heard a strange voice calling to me. Before our truck had rolled to a stop, I spotted an old advertising thermometer still attached to the skeletal remains of the shop. As I came closer and could see the thermometer better, I realized the voice was coming from it and was saying "Take me home!" This old piece was a bit on the rusty side, but its lettering was readable and it was still in working condition. It was an advertising thermometer for the Johnson Brothers Coffin Shop. Since I was a teenager, ghost stories about their old place had abounded. I still have this first find and have seen very few since then.

As with clocks and calendars, thermometers serve as yet another product reminder that the general public uses on a constant basis. The majority of advertising thermometers use the mercury-in-glass method of measuring temperature. The glass thermometer is surrounded by art work and advertising messages. Coca-Cola produced great thermometers and these are usually easy to find. However, be aware that there are many reproductions on the market. Being a reproduction doesn't reduce the artful impact, but it does reduce the price substantially. Most often these thermometers were give-aways to the retailer that came with merchandise to be sold. Some were made to be given or sold directly to the general public. When you purchase one, make sure the glass tube has not been cracked or broken. To be honest, I have bought a few that were not in working condition simply because I admired the advertising art. You may think that a bit of rust means that the piece is old. But rust has not been there long if it is bright red and will wipe off. Advertising thermometers command an area of advertising memorabilia that cannot be overlooked because of their combination of practicality and artful beauty.

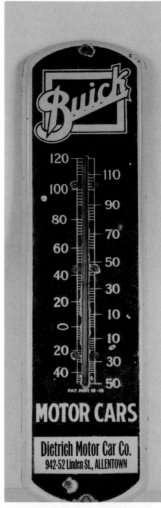

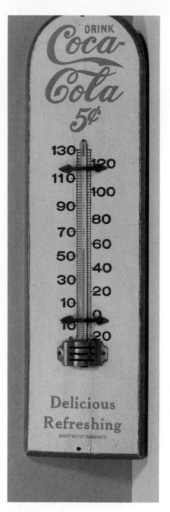

Buick/MOTOR CARS
1915, 7¼" x 27", porcelain
thermometer. $275.00(B)

Coca-Cola/5¢
1905, 4" x 15", wooden
thermometer. $675.00(B)

Coca-Cola/100TH ANNIVERSARY
Metal thermometer. $25.00(C)

**Left: Coca-Cola/
DIE-CUT DEC. 25, 1923, BOTTLE**
Produced in 1933, embossed tin
thermometer. $110.00(B)

**Right: Coca-Cola/
DIE-CUT DEC. 25, 1923, BOTTLE**
Produced in 1931, embossed tin
thermometer. $210.00(B)

Coca-Cola/TWO BOTTLES
1941, embossed tin thermometer.
$475.00(B)

Coca-Cola/SINGLE BOTTLE
1938, embossed tin thermometer.
$250.00(B)

Coca-Cola/
DRINK COCA-COLA IN BOTTLES
1939, 10" x 14", mirror with thermometer.
$450.00(B)

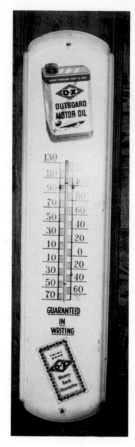

D-X/
OUTBOARD MOTOR OIL
Metal thermometer.
$65.00(C)

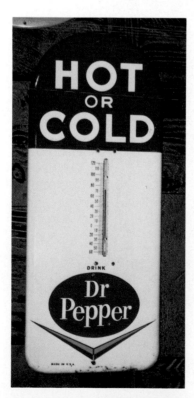

Dr Pepper/HOT OR COLD
Painted metal thermome-
ter. $45.00(C)

Dr Pepper/WHEN HUNGRY...
Metal thermometer. $65.00(C)

Double Cola/YOU'LL LIKE IT BETTER
Metal thermometer. $45.00(C)

Double Cola/MAKE IT A DOUBLE…
Metal thermometer. $75.00(C)

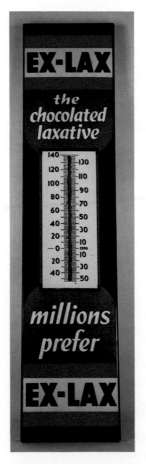

Du Pont/DENATURED ALCOHOL
8" x 38¾", painted metal thermometer. $75.00(B)

Ex-Lax/THE CHOCOLATED LAXATIVE
Thermometer. $90.00(B)

Freeman/HEADBOLT ENGINE HEATER
6" x 15", painted metal thermometer. $80.00(B)

Frostie/DRINK...
Painted metal thermometer. $25.00(C)

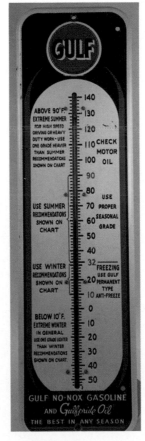

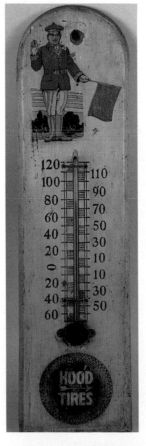

Goodyear/PERLEY W. LOUD
3¼" x 11½", wooden thermometer. $50.00(B)

Gulf/NO-NOX
7½" x 26½", painted tin thermometer. $240.00(B)

Hood Tires/MAN WITH FLAG
4" x 15", wooden thermometer. $265.00(B)

Johnson Bros/FUNERAL DIRECTORS
8½" x 38½", metal thermometer. $75.00(C)

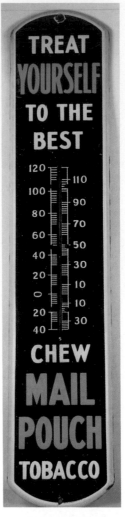

Mail Pouch/TREAT YOURSELF...
8" x 38¾", porcelain thermometer. $85.00(B)

**Marvells/
THE CIGARETTE OF QUALITY**
Metal thermometer.
$35.00(C)

Merrill/TRANSPORT COMPANY
15" diameter with tire & tube holding center thermometer. $200.00(B)

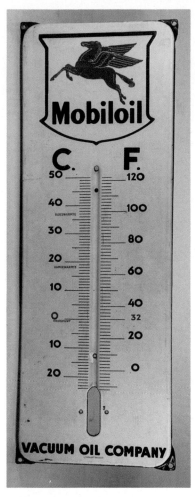

**Mobiloil/
VACUUM OIL COMPANY**
8" x 23", porcelain ther-
mometer. $250.00(B)

Nash/P. K. WILLIAMS
7½" x 15", plastic thermometer. $5.00(B)

Mobilgas/FRIENDLY SERVICE
4¼" x 34½", porcelain thermometer. $240.00(B)

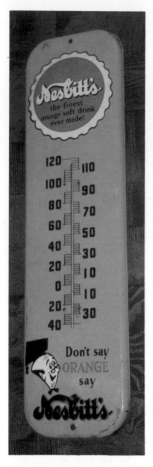

Nesbitt's/DON'T SAY ORANGE…
Metal thermometer. $55.00(C)

Nesbitt's/PICTURE OF BOTTLE AND LOGO
Metal thermometer. $95.00(C)

**NuGrape/
BOTTLE SHAPED**
Metal thermometer.
$75.00(C)

Oilzum/THE CHOICE OF CHAMPION RACE DRIVERS
7½" x 15", painted tin thermometer. $425.00(B)

Crush/THIRSTY
Tin thermometer. $35.00(C)

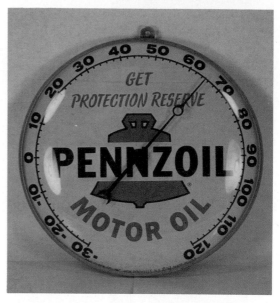

Pennsylvania Motor Oil/AMALIE
9" diameter, glass faced thermometer.
$65.00(B)

Pennzoil/GET PROTECTION RESERVE
12" diameter, glass faced thermometer.
$160.00(B)

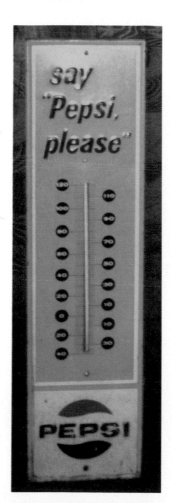

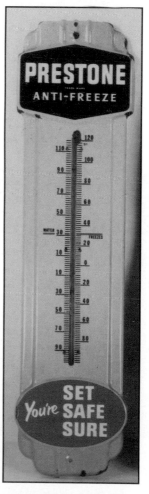

Pepsi-Cola/SAY PEPSI PLEASE
Tin thermometer. $35.00(C)

Pepsi-Cola/WITH BOTTLE CAPS
Reproduction metal thermometer. $35.00(C)

Prestone/ANTI-FREEZE
1940s, 8¾" x 36", porcelain
thermometer. $100.00(B)

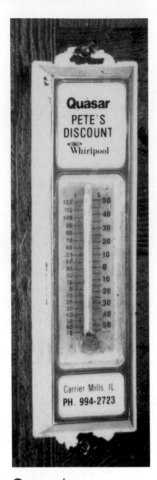

**Quasar/
PETE'S DISCOUNT**
Metal thermometer.
$25.00(C)

Salem/REFRESHES YOUR TASTE
Metal thermometer. $25.00(C)

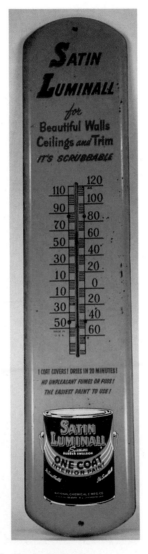

**Satin Luminall/
FOR BEAUTIFUL WALLS...**
8½" x 38½", painted metal
thermometer. $35.00(B)

Royal Crown Cola/RC
Metal thermometer. $50.00(C)

**7-Up/
FIRST AGAINST THIRST**
6¼" x 17¾", plastic ther-
mometer. $25.00(C)

Shaler Rislone/ASK ABOUT...
9½" x 25", painted metal
thermometer. $25.00(B)

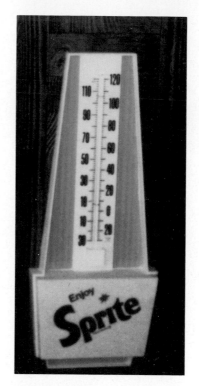

Sprite/ENJOY
Metal thermometer.$25.00(C)

Squirt/
NEVER AN AFTER THIRST
Metal thermometer.
$35.00(C)

Sun Crest/BOTTLE SHAPED
Metal thermometer. $60.00(C)

Texaco/ROY EL GOURLEY
12" diameter, glass faced thermometer. $500.00(B)

Tops/SMOKELESS TREAT
Thermometer. $25.00(C)

Tums/QUICK RELIEF...
4" x 9", thermometer marked
made in U.S.A. $50.00(B)

Union Farmer's Gin/
H A BOON, MANAGER, PHONE 32, PORTAGEVILLE, MO
10¼" x 8¼", painted glass scene thermometer.
$30.00(C)

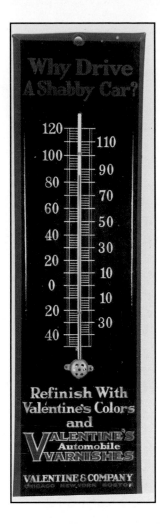

**Valentine & Co./
WHY DRIVE A SHABBY CAR?**
5½" x 20", celluloid thermometer. $110.00(B)

Vantage/BUY A PACK TODAY
Metal thermometer. $25.00(C)

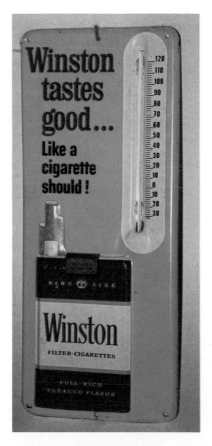

Winston/THE TASTE IS TOPS...
Metal thermometer. $25.00(C)

**Winston/TASTES GOOD...LIKE
A CIGARETTE SHOULD**
6" x 13½", embossed metal
thermometer. $28.00(D)

**Winston/TASTES GOOD...LIKE
A CIGARETTE SHOULD**
(Has Surgeon General's
warning) 6" x 13½", embossed
metal thermometer.
$30.00(C)

TRAYS

Used extensively in soda fountains, restaurants, and the corner bar, the advertising tray is a familiar and utilitarian piece of advertising memorabilia. Food and beverage companies have over the years produced a vast amount of serving trays. Unquestionably, the most famous and prolific producer of these is Coca-Cola. A Coke tray can take you back decades to a time when life traveled at a different pace. Coke's advertising campaigns have met with great success in the past partly due to the fact that they have employed the talents of famous artists. These artist's expertise combined with some outstanding celebrity endorsements have produced a tremendous amount of trays in wonderful shapes, sizes, styles, and colors. One of the problems with collecting Coca-Cola trays is that these artist's styles have been so popular, demand for them has produced an overwhelming body of reproductions. Of course the fact that it is a reproduction does not lessen the artistic impact as a decorative piece, but it most certainly affects the price. Because of this reproduction problem if you are going to become a serious collector of Coca-Cola items you need to do a fair amount of studying to really know what you are purchasing. Because this book is an overall look at advertising memorabilia, I won't go into detail on this matter. There are several good books on the market today that have researched Coca-Cola advertising history and if you want to begin collecting early Coke advertising art, I recommend that you educate yourself before purchasing items represented as authentic. But if your aim is to decorate and you want some great art — reproductions are an inexpensive route to take, and they look great!

Since advertising trays were, as a rule, used in a serving capacity, most of the products depicted were food, beverages, ice-cream, and confections. You can also find advertising trays from cigarette companies and mineral water producers as well as advertising premiums for various stores and products. Souvenir trays were available from almost every state in the Union, usually focusing on some well-known vacation spot. The easiest to find, however, will be for soft drinks. Whether petite tip trays used to coerce a patron out of a gratuity, or full size serving trays, every time your order arrived the company that produced the tray received repetitive advertising all for the cost of one single tray.

Blatz/OLD HEIDELBERG
13¼" x 10½" metal tray. $97.00(D)

Christian Feigenspan Brewing Co./
WOMAN WITH RED RIBBON IN HAIR
13¼" diameter, metal tray. $60.00(D)

Coca-Cola/
HAMILTON KING, THE Coca-Cola GIRL
1910, metal tray. $300.00(B)

Coca-Cola/ELAINE
1916, metal tray. $140.00(B)

Coca-Cola/TOPLESS WOMAN
1908, lithographed, hard-to-find, metal tray.
$4,300.00(B)

Coca-Cola/HILDA CLARK
1903, 9¼" diameter, hard-to-find, metal
tray. $1,100.00(B)

Coca-Cola/SAILOR GIRL
1940, metal tray. $800.00(B)

Coca-Cola/BETTY
1914, oval metal tray. $260.00(B)

Coca-Cola/HAMILTON KING GIRL
1913, oval metal tray. $260.00(B)

Coca-Cola/CURB SERVICE
1927, metal tray. $1,400.00(B)

Coca-Cola/SODA JERK
1928, metal tray. $725.00(B)

Coca-Cola/TWO GIRLS IN CONVERTIBLE
1942, metal tray. $360.00(B)

Coca-Cola/YELLOW GIRL
1920, oval metal tray. $160.00(B)

Coca-Cola/GIRL IN AFTERNOON
1938, metal tray. $120.00(B)

Coca-Cola/EXPOSITION GIRL
1909, oval metal tray. $650.00(B)

Coca-Cola/HILDA WITH ROSES
1901, 9¼" diameter, metal tray. $1,000.00(B)

Coca-Cola/ICE SKATER
1941, metal tray. $160.00(B)

Coca-Cola/RED-HEAD GIRL
1950–52, fairly scarce, metal tray. $200.00(B)

Coca-Cola/RUNNING GIRL
1937, metal tray. $300.00(B)

Coca-Cola/FRANCIS DEE
1933, metal tray. $950.00(B)

Coca-Cola/GIRL IN BATHING SUIT AND HAT
1930, metal tray. $180.00(B)

Coca-Cola/MADGE EVANS
1935, metal tray. $180.00(B)

Coca-Cola/SWIMSUIT GIRL WITH GLASS
1929, metal tray. $150.00(B)

Coca-Cola/GIRL IN PINK
1922, metal tray. $1,450.00(B)

Coca-Cola/WEISSMULLER
1934, metal tray. $900.00(B)

Coca-Cola/GIRL WITH STRAW
1927, metal tray. $625.00(B)

Coca-Cola/FISHING BOY WITH PUP
1931, metal tray. $650.00(B)

Coca-Cola/FOXSKIN FUR GIRL
1925, metal tray. $100.00(B)

Coca-Cola/GIRL WITH MENU
1950s, 10½" x 13¼", metal tray. $55.00(C)

Erlanger Beer/CLASSIC 1893
13" x 10½" metal tray. $5.50(D)

The Fair's Millenary/OPENING
1905, 5" x 3½", tip tray. $10.00(B)

Frederick's Premium Beer/BREWED
With PURE ARTESIAN WELL WATER
13¼" diameter, metal tray. $75.00(D)

Liberty/ICE CREAM
Rectangular tray. $13.00(D)

Maxwell House Coffee/"SINCE 1892"
15" x 12½", metal tray. $15.00(D)

Miller High Life/
THE CHAMPAGNE OF BOTTLED BEER
12" diameter, metal tray. $48.00(D)

Niagara Falls, New York/
SCENES OF NIAGARA FALLS
13¾" x 9¾", metal tray. $3.00(D)

Old Reading Brewery, Inc./READING, PENNSYLVANIA
12" diameter, metal tray. $30.00(D)

Rock Spring/SPARKLING WATER
12" diameter, metal tray. $7.50(D)

Satin/TURKISH CIGARETTES, 20 FOR 15cts.
13¾" diameter, metal tray. $32.00(D)

7-Up/THE UNCOLA
12" diameter, metal tray. $7.00(D)

Standard Brewing Co./TRU AGE
12" diameter, metal tray. $60.00(D)

Stollwerck/CHOCOLATE AND COCOA
5⅛" diameter, tip tray. $15.00(B)

Thompson's/ICE CREAM
Round metal tray. $30.00(B)

MISCELLANEOUS

Every book should have a catch-all chapter and this is it! There is a vast body of advertising memorabilia that is designed to hold, contain, dispense, display, and otherwise call attention to products. The goal of advertising is, after all, to sell a product. Have you ever watched children in the cookie aisle of a grocery store? Do they want a product because of the contents, or are they scanning for the best looking package, one that they know and are familiar with. Advertising pieces are designed to establish contact with the public and build a reputation for quality merchandise. For this reason trademarks are used so the public can immediately relate to the product. Even though some pieces may not advertise a specific product, a logo or trademark is very useful for keeping the company name out on the market. Then when displaying the merchandise at the actual point of purchase, the artist can be specific for the product. To be a successful advertisement the piece must first attract your attention and then make you curious enough to stop and look it over. It must then relay the idea that you need it, it is quality merchandise, and you should try it now.

Cracker, cookie, and peanut jars are of special interest to me. Also among my favorites, probably because they are getting hard to find, are advertising crocks. This collection of advertising miscellaneous is as varied in pieces as it is in prices. Some of these collectibles are most common place and others are rare. Packaging sells and for this reason it is usually not difficult to find good containers with good art work at affordable prices! A container advertising a product no longer available will command a higher price, of course, than one still in production. Check for cracks, breaks, and repairs before arriving at a decision to make a purchase. Miscellaneous covers a broad field and, like me, most collectors will pick up almost any good buy even if it is not in their particular field of interest. This will give you good trading material when you do find that item you want. Whatever your interest in this varied field, I hope you enjoy this pictorial reflection on advertising memorabilia.

Alka-Seltzer/DISPLAY BOX
25¼" x 6¼" x 6¼", paper-linen. $5.00(B)

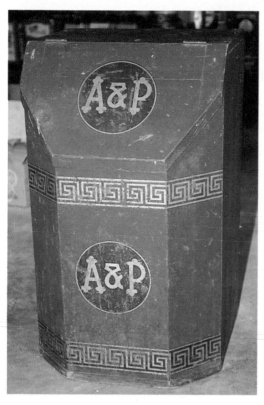

Alka-Seltzer
12" x 9½", metal display. $30.00(B)

A&P
30" tall, wooden tea bin. $210.00(B)

American
3" x 2⅜", cloth sleeve patch. $5.00(B)

Amrhein's Bread/ASK FOR AMRHEIN'S BREAD, IT'S FRESHER
26" x 3", painted metal door push. $45.00(D)

Baby Ruth/TAPE DISPENSER
10½" x 2", porcelain with paper labels. $25.00(B)

Anteek Beer/FIGURAL
22½" tall, composition figural display.
$300.00(B)

**The Badger Mutual Fire Insurance Co./
BADGER FIGURINE**
Cast metal paperweight. $55.00(B)

Balkan Sobranie/TURKISH CIGARETTES
6¼" x 2⅞" x 1⅛" box. $25.00(B)

Barber Greene/
MODEL TOY
6½" x 12", metal toy
grain loader. $170.00(B)

Beacon Shoes/LIGHTHOUSE ON ROCK
6¼" x 10½", composition logo. $40.00(D)

Beefeater Gin/THE IMPORTED ONE
8½" x 17", wood and composition back bar
statue. $75.00(B)

Blatz/BLATZ CAN MAN HOLDING MUG OF BEER
6½" x 10½", metal and plastic figurine.
$100.00(D)

Blatz/BLATZ BOTTLE MAN HOLDING MUG OF BEER
6¾" x 15½", glass and plastic figurine. $100.00(D)

Burpee Seed Co./ BURPEE SEEDS GROW
17½" x 21½", cloth seed sack.
$5.00(D)

Campfire/MARSHMALLOWS
Round tin with lid. $12.00(D)

Camel/VULCANIZING PATCHES
Cardboard and tin. $6.00(D)

Chesterfield/ FLAT FIFTIES
5½" x 4½", hinged cigarette tin. $15.00(B)

Cape County Milling Company/ COLONIAL
Reproduction (1971), woven cotton flour bag. $5.00(D)

Carter Carburetor/LIGHT UP
13½" x 27½", milk glass globe and cast iron display piece. $500.00(B)

Chevron/SUPREME GASOLINE
2¾" diameter, cloth sleeve patch. $10.00(B)

Citgo
2⅜" square, cloth sleeve patch. $5.00(B)

Coca-Cola/DRINK
1912–13, clear glass tumbler, etched. $675.00(B)

Coca-Cola/IN BOTTLES
22½" wide x 35" tall x 12" deep, cooler, new. $185.00(B)

Coca-Cola
1896 ceramic dispenser marked The Wheeling Pottery Co. $5,200.00(B)

Coca-Cola/DRINK
1920s, syrup bottle. $1,200.00(B)

Coca-Cola/50th ANNIVERSARY
Cigarette case. $300.00(B)

Coca-Cola/PICTURE OF BOTTLE AND GLASS IN CENTER
Knowles china sandwich plate. $150.00(B)

Coca-Cola/HAVE A COKE
1950s, plastic and metal
door pull handle. $160.00(B)

Left: Coca-Cola/THE COCA-COLA CO., ATLANTA
1916–19, wooden 5 gal. keg. $170.00(B)
Right: Coca-Cola/THE COCA-COLA CO., ATLANTA
1916–19, wooden 10 gal. keg. $40.00(B)

**Coca-Cola/
SELTZER BOTTLE**
Acid etched green glass.
$200.00(B)

**Coca-Cola/
SELTZER BOTTLE**
37 oz., painted clear glass.
$150.00(B)

Coca-Cola/MINIATURE 6-PAK
1950s. $85.00(B)

Coca-Cola/BELL SHAPED
Pewter tumbler. $300.00(B)

Coca-Cola/ICE COLD
Green Vernonware bowl. $450.00(B)

Coca-Cola/BOTTLE TOPPER
1927, 8" x 10½", printed by U.S. Printing and Litho Co. $2,000.00(B)

Coca-Cola/DRINK ICE COLD
1950s, 12" x 9½" x 17", cooler radio. $550.00(B)

Coca-Cola/DRINK ICE COLD
1950s, 12" x 9½" x 17", cooler radio reproduction. $125.00(D)

Coca-Cola/DRINK ICE COLD
1950s small crystal radio. $240.00(B)

Coca-Cola/DRINK ICE COLD
1950s miniature music box, plays "Let me call you sweetheart." $120.00(B)

Coca-Cola/DRINK
1950s cargo toy truck with working headlights and taillights. $225.00(B)

Coca-Cola/SPRITE BOY
1940s toy truck. $250.00(B)

**Colonial Bread/
COLONIAL IS GOOD BREAD**
36" x 3½", embossed painted
metal door push. $35.00(D)

Comstock Bros./UTICA, NY
9" tall, crock jug. $130.00(B)

Consolidated Ice Co./WINTER SCENE
Dresser mirror. $80.00(B)

Crescent/MACARONI
Tin with handles. $65.00(D)

Crispo/LILY SODAS
Soda crackers tin with lid. $31.00(D)

D-X
5½" x 4", license plate reflector. $10.00(B)

Dairy Brand/NEW YORK VANILLA ICE CREAM
Half gallon can with lid. $20.00(C)

Dobbs/FIFTH AVENUE HATS, NY
4" x 3½" x 2½", black, paper covered cardboard box with red plastic insert, gift certificate premium returned to store for hat. $45.00(D)

Diamond Dyes/FAST COLORS/DOMESTIC FANCY DYEING
Late 1800 to early 1900 original oak cabinet with tin litho. depicting the life of a woman from birth to old age, known as an evolution cabinet. $850.00(B)

Edgeworth/EXTRA HIGH GRADE
Pipe tobacco tins. Small $12.00(D); Medium $19.00(D)

Edison/NAME YOUR CAR...
Mazda counter display box.
$300.00–$750.00(B)

Esso/WATCH YOUR SAVINGS GROW
4¾" square, embossed glass block
bank. $55.00(B)

Esso/BANK
6½" tall, plastic bank.
$110.00(B)

**Falls City Beer/IT'S PASTEUR-
IZED, IT'S BITTER FREE**
7¾" x 9¾", paper, 6-pack take-
out bag with handle. $7.00(D)

Franklin/GLASS & MIRROR MANUFACTURERS
3⅜" diameter, pocket mirror. $10.00(B)

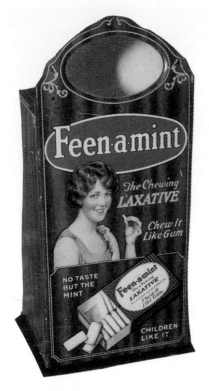

Feen-a-mint/
THE CHEWING LAXATIVE
Counter display holder.
$350.00(B)

Game Finecut Tobacco/ BIRD SCENE
11½" x 6½" x 8" tobacco tin. $285.00(B)
Manufactured by "Jno. J. Bagley E. Co,
Detroit, Mich."

Getty
4½" x 2⅞", cloth sleeve patch. $5.00(B)

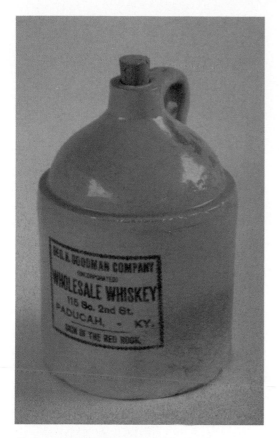

**Geo. H. Goodman Company/
WHOLESALE WHISKEY**
1 gallon, crock jug. $150.00(C)

Gilmer/MOULDED RUBBER
Fan belt box. $300.00-$750.00(B)

Gordon's/FRESH POTATO CHIPS
11¼" tall, round tin, one lb. $55.00(B)

**Gordon's/
"TRUCKS SERVING THE BEST"**
7½" dia. x 7¾", clear glass store jar with
metal lid. $125.00(C)

Gulf
2½" x 2¼", cloth sleeve patch. $10.00(B)

HACO/LOLITA TALCUM POWDER
4¼" x 7" x 19", oval metal container. $135.00(D)

Half & Half/BURLEY AND BRIGHT TOBACCO
3" x 4¼" x 1", tobacco tin. $4.50(D)

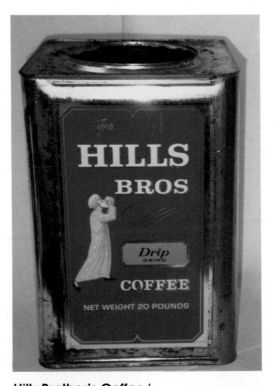

Hills Brother's Coffee/ DRIP GRIND COFFEE
9½" x 9½" x 13", 20lb., tin container. $20.00(D)

Hires/ROOT BEER
22" tall, dispenser. $200.00(B)

**Illinois Agricultural Mutual Insurance Co./
ILLINOIS FARM BUREAUS**
3¾" x 4½", license plate attachment, porcelain.
$80.00(B)

Indianapolis Speedway Flag
17" x 17", silk. $55.00(B)

**Jack Daniel's/
GOLD MEDAL OLD NO. 7**
Crockery jug. $45.00(D)

John D. Jr./HAND SOAP
3lb. tin. $18.00(D)

**Johnston Milwaukee/
CHARM SODA CRACKERS**
One lb. box. $12.00(D)

Jolly Pops/THOSE GOOD SUCKERS
9½" x 20", metal dispenser.
$80.00(B)

Knapsack /MATCHES
10" diameter x 10½" tall, wood,
metal, and glass match dispenser.
$550.00(B)

Kool/MENTHOL MAGIC
Metal cigarette holder.
$35.00(C)

**L.S. DuBois/
WHOLESALE DRUGGIST**
1 gallon, crockery jug.
$135.00(C)

Lance/75th ANNIVERSARY
Clear cracker jar. $75.00(D)

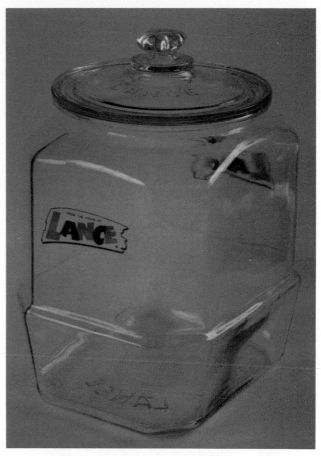

Lance/FROM THE HOUSE OF LANCE
7" x 8½" x 13", clear glass store jar. $65.00(C)
(Lance embossed on both sides of handle on
top and on bottom of jar.)

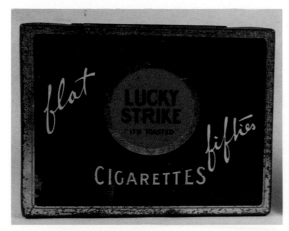

Lucky Strike/FLAT FIFTIES
5½" x 4½", hinged cigarette tin. $15.00(B)

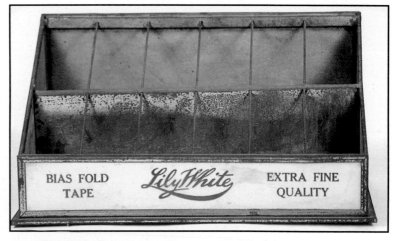

Lily White/BIAS FOLD TAPE
15" x 8¼" x 8", metal display. $25.00(B)

Magnolia Brand/CONDENSED MILK
19" wide x 7" tall x 13" deep, wooden box, debossed black painted letters. $25.00(B)

Marlboro/SOLD HERE
Metal cigarette holder. $40.00(C)

Mason's/OLD FASHIONED ROOT BEER
10" x 10", cardboard display with bottle. $75.00(D)

Master Trucks Inc./TRUCK
7" wide x 5½" tall x 2¾" deep, cast iron, embossed lettering ink, well marked "Master Trucks Inc. Chicago, USA." $210.00(B)

Merion/HAIR NET
Metal box with mirror
on lid. $75.00(D)

Meadow Gold/VANILLA ICE CREAM
Half-gallon, round tin. $9.00(D)

Michelin/MICHELIN MAN
1940s, 6" x 4¾", molded plastic ashtray.
$75.00(B)

Merrick's/SIX CORD SPOOL COTTON
Wood and glass cabinet. $975.00(D)

Mr. Peanut/MR. PEANUT HEAD
7½" x 12", yellow and blue plastic store jar.
$45.00(C)

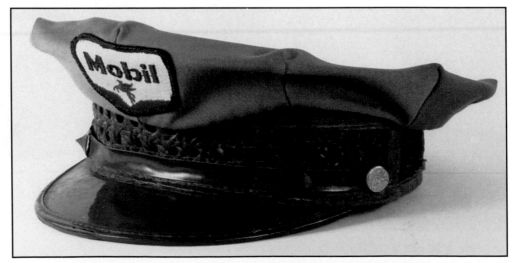

Mr. Peanut/MR. PEANUT FIGURE
1970s, 12½" tall, plastic figural peanut butter maker. $30.00(C)

Mobil
3⅛" x 1¼", cloth sleeve patch. $5.00(B)

Mobil
Attendant's hat, all original. $175.00(B)

Mobilgas/TOY
2½" x 9", tin, Ford tanker truck. $175.00(B)

Mobilgas/SPECIAL
Restored gas pump.
$2200.00(D)

**Mobiloil/
GARGOYLE MOBILOIL "E"**
Metal can. $30.00(D)

Modern Girl/BEAUTIFUL STOCKINGS
7½" x 9¾" x 1½", stocking box . $12.00(D)

Mojud/THIGH-MOLD STRETCH TOP
11" x 11½", garter belt display. $75.00(D)

Mojud/THE SHEER ALL NYLON STOCKINGS...
13" x 12" x 7", supp-hose display. $100.00(D)

Monarch/GREEN TEA
Tin with lid. $9.00(D)

Munsing Wear/FASHION BOOKS...
12" x 14", counter display. $800.00(B)

New Era/POTATO CHIPS
Round tin. $45.00(B)

Nikolai/DANCING RUSSIAN
Figural display. $50.00(B*)

**No Company Name/
GET EM HOT**
21" tall, peanut dispenser.
$165.00(B)

No Company/TOY GAS PUMP
6½" tall, cast iron. $400.00(B)

No Company/COUNTRY STORE
20" wide x 36" high x 13" deep, merchandise vendor. $330.00(B)

Obermeyer & Leibmann's/BOTTLED BEER
43" tall, beer cart. $1500.00(B)

OCB/ROLL YOUR OWN...
Cigarette papers holder. $30.00(C)

Old Crow/OLD CROW
3½" x 11½", composition figural advertising logo. $75.00(D)

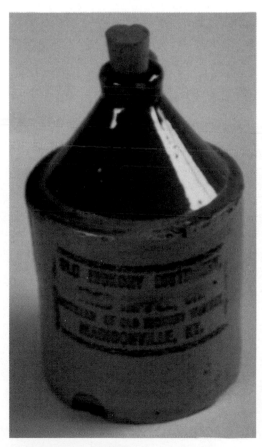

**Old Hickory Distillery/
MADISONVILLE, KENTUCKY**
Half-gallon, crock jug. $150.00(C)

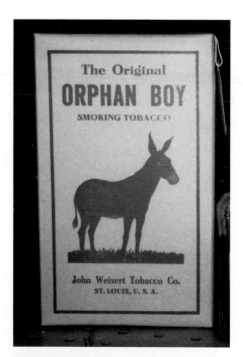

**Orphan Boy/
SMOKING TOBACCO**
Cardboard box. $7.00(D)

Parker Brothers Inc./
THE WONDERFUL GAME OF OZ
1921, complete game in box.
$160.00(B) Marked:"Parker
Brothers Inc. Salem, MASS,
New York, London," "regis-
tered U. S. Patent office."

Pepsi-Cola/IDEAL
Drink cooler. $350.00(D)

Pepsi-Cola/HAVE A PEPSI
Plastic and metal fountain dispenser. $175.00(D)

Pepsi-Cola/SAY "PEPSI, PLEASE"
Painted metal soda fountain black board.
$35.00(D)

Phillips 66/SILVER ANNIVERSARY
3½" diameter, paperweight mirror. $120.00(B)

Planters/SALTED PEANUTS
8½" diameter, 9¾" tall, round tin. $5.00(B)

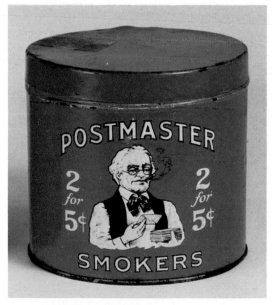

Postmaster/SMOKERS
5¼" tall x 5" diameter, round tin.
$25.00(B)

Postum/HEALTH FIRST
Tin string holder. $280.00(B)

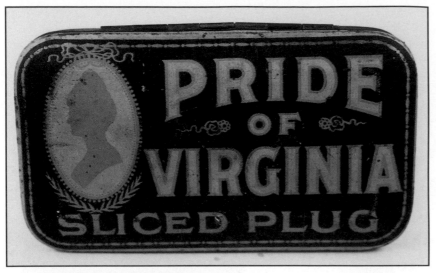

Pride of Virginia/SLICED PLUG
Rectangular tobacco tin. $10.00(B)

Prince Albert/CRIMP CUT
Pipe tobacco tin. $9.00(D)

Putnam/FADELESS DYES
Tin display box. $135.00(D)

Pulver/CHEWING GUM
8½" x 20" tall, dispenser. $625.00(B)

Ray Cotton Company/TRUCK
8" wide x 3¾" tall x 3" deep, cast iron embossed lettering ink well, marked — Ray Cotton Company/Franklin, Mass. Agents Cotton Mills Waste Association. $80.00(B)

R. C. Wallace & Co./GROCERS
1 gallon, crock jug. $135.00(D)

Rexall/FROM THE REXALL STORE
4¼" diameter x 4¾" tall, embossed clear glass bowl. $20.00(B)

**Rosemary Foods/
THE HIGHEST STANDARD...**
15" wide x 14" high x 34" deep, wagon. $40.00(B)

Royal Baking Powder/BOX
14¾" wide x 8½" tall x 7¾" deep, wooden box, black debossed lettering front and back. $20.00(B)

Royal Crown/COLA
Metal cooler. $65.00(C)

Ruff-Stuff/THE SANDPAPER THAT SATISFIES
12" wide x 23" tall x 14" deep, painted metal display. $100.00(B)

S. J. Tuft/GIRL WITH BROOM
Die cut cardboard dust pan. $20.00(B*)

"Salada Tea"/DELICIOUS FLAVOR
34" x 3½", porcelain door push. $65.00(D)

Salem/CHANGE TO SALEM
10" x 10", rubber with astro turf change pad. $9.00(D)

Seagram's/NUMBER 7
8" x 7", glass serving pitcher with handle. $10.00(D)

Schrader/TIRE GAUGE
1920–30, 6" x 14¾", can used
to store tire gauges within
hinged door. $160.00(B)

7-Up/FRESHEN UP
31½" x 3", metal door push. $55.00(D)

**7-Up/FRESHEN UP
WITH 7-UP**
5" x 8½", paper bottle
capper. $12.00(D)

Sergeant's/DOG CARE PRODUCTS
14½" x 25¼", cardboard display with
movable leg on dog. $125.00(D)

Shell
2" square, cloth sleeve patch. $5.00(B)

**Shell/
TOOTSIE TOY**
1¾" x 6", tanker
truck, pressed
steel. $55.00(B)

Simoniz/GIVES LASTING BEAUTY...
Display. $150.00(B)

Snowdrift/SWEETENED FANCY SHRED COCONUT
12" dia. x 14½" tall, tin. $25.00(B)

Sinclair/MARX TOY
18½" long, tanker truck. $650.00(B)

Snow-King/PEANUTS, CARAMEL, NOUGAT
10" x 7¾" x 2", candy bar box. $28.00(D)

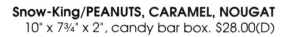

StaCool Oil/KEEPS THE MOTOR COOL!
1 gal., tin. $29.00(D)

**Starr Service/
WE INVITE YOU TO DEAL AND TRADE...**
12" x 24", salesman sample box with
reverse painted glass advertisements.
$80.00(B)

**Sterling Beer/MELLOW
STERLING BEER**
4¾" x 14¾", metal figural
bell. $60.00(D)

Sunbeam/WHITE STROEHMANN
Door push. $165.00(D)

Sunoco
2¾" x 2", cloth sleeve patch. $5.00(B)

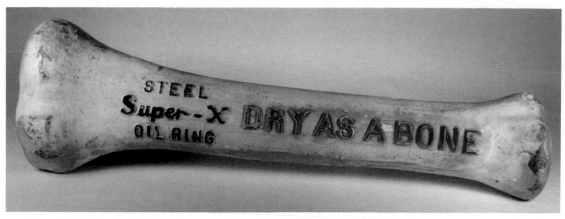

Super-X/DRY AS A BONE
24" long, rare, papier maché bone. $200.00–$600.00(B*)

Sure Shot/CHEWING TOBACCO
Rectangular store tin. $650.00(B)

Sweet Cuba/CHEWING TOBACCO
Tin with hinged lid. $450.00(B)

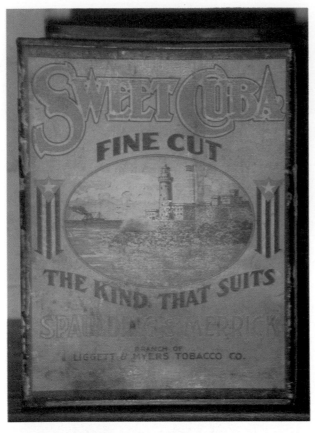

Sweet Cuba/GENUINE...FINE CUT
Tobacco tin. $39.00(D)

Sweet Cuba/FINE CUT
Tobacco pail. $14.00(D)

Sylcraft/UNDERGARMENTS OF QUALITY
11¼" x 11½" x 1½", undergarment box.
$22.00(D)

TWA/AIRPLANE
10" x 6", metal ashtray. $125.00(B)

Texaco/SUPREME GASOLINE
2¼" x 2", cloth sleeve patch. $5.00(B)

Texaco
2½" diameter, cloth sleeve patch. $5.00(B)

Texaco/TOY TANKER
5" x 26½", plastic motorized,
dealer offer toy, with box.
$180.00(B)

Texaco/FIRE CHIEF GASOLINE
5" tall x 11" long, promotion celluloid hat. $25.00(B)

Texaco/FIRE CHIEF GASOLINE
8" tall, plastic firechief's hat. $60.00(B)

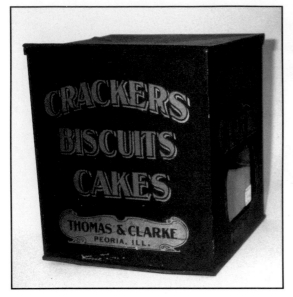

Thomas & Clark/
CRACKERS, BISCUITS, CAKES
7½" x 7½" x 9", tin container. $125.00(D)

Tidewater/FLYING A
14" wide x 6¼" tall x 11½" deep, metal credit card machine.
$75.00(B)

Tiger/CHEWING TOBACCO
6" x 4" x 2½", chewing tobacco tin. $44.00(D)

UMWA/MINER'S HAT
15" x 17½", salesman sample miner's hat,
wood on metal. $35.00(B)

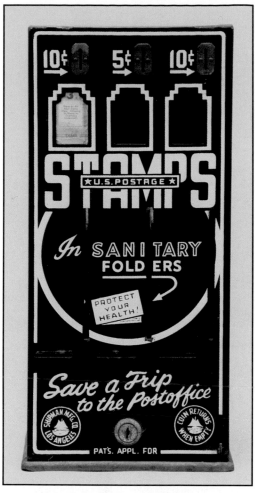

U.S. Postal System/
STAMPS IN SANITARY FOLDERS
7¼" x 16", porcelain front with metal
back stamp dispenser. $85.00(B)

U.S. Postal System/
STAMPS
8½" x 15", painted
white metal stamp
dispenser with cast
iron base. $65.00(B)

U. S. School Garden/RAISED'EM MYSELF...
Framed poster. $150.00(B)

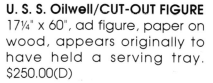

U. S. S. Oilwell/CUT-OUT FIGURE
17¼" x 60", ad figure, paper on
wood, appears originally to
have held a serving tray.
$250.00(D)

Velvet/PIPE & CIGARETTE
Tobacco tin. $12.00(D)

**Western Union/
BELL PAGE**
3½" x 5¾", porcelain.
$50.00(B)

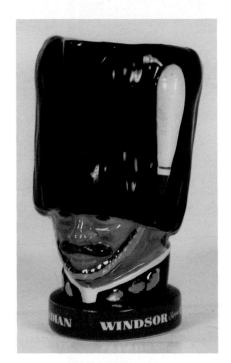

**W. Schneider/
WHOLESALE WINE & LIQUOR CO.**
1 gallon, crockery jug. $95.00(D)

Windsor/SUPREME
4" diameter x 8½" tall, figural
pitcher, ceramic. $20.00(B)

White Owl/SQUIRES
Cigar tin. $18.00(D)

Winner/CUT PLUG
4" tall, hinged tobacco pail. $60.00(B)

Whiz/PATCH OUTFIT
Display. $300.00(B)

Wrigley's/SURE ITS WRIGLEY'S
13" x 13", counter display. $350.00(B)

Zig-Zag/CIGARETTE PAPERS
6" tall, dispenser. $65.00(B)

INDEX

Schroeder's
ANTIQUES
Price Guide

. . . is the #1 best-selling antiques & collectibles value guide on the market today, and here's why . . .

Schroeder's
ANTIQUES
Price Guide

OUR #1 BEST SELLER!

Identification & Values Of Over 50,000 Antiques & Collectibles

8½ x 11, 608 Pages, $12.95

- *More than 300 advisors, well-known dealers, and top-notch collectors work together with our editors to bring you accurate information regarding pricing and identification.*

- *More than 45,000 items in almost 500 categories are listed along with hundreds of sharp original photos that illustrate not only the rare and unusual, but the common, popular collectibles as well.*

- *Each large close-up shot shows important details clearly. Every subject is represented with histories and background information, a feature not found in any of our competitors' publications.*

- *Our editors keep abreast of newly-developing trends, often adding several new categories a year as the need arises.*

If it merits the interest of today's collector, you'll find it in *Schroeder's.* And you can feel confident that the information we publish is up to date and accurate. Our advisors thoroughly check each category to spot inconsistencies, listings that may not be entirely reflective of market dealings, and lines too vague to be of merit. Only the best of the lot remains for publication.

Without doubt, you'll find
SCHROEDER'S ANTIQUES PRICE GUIDE
the only one to buy for
reliable information and values.

COLLECTOR BOOKS
A Division of Schroeder Publishing Co., Inc.